3/94

How to Become a Virgin

Quentin Crisp

How to
Become a Virgin

St. Martin's Press
New York

Library of Congress Cataloging in Publication Data

Crisp, Quentin.
How to become a virgin.

1. Crisp, Quentin—Biography. 2. Authors,
English—20th century—Biography. 3. Homosexuals,
Male—Great Britain—Biography. I. Title.
PR6005.R65Z464   306.7'6'0924   [B]   81-16528
ISBN 0-312-39543-4   AACR2

Contents

The Beginning

I am not a drop-out; I was never in.

I have not spent my life hacking my way through the constraints of a bourgeois existence. I was always free – appallingly free.

For my first fifty years I was like someone standing alone in a landscape which led to infinite possibilities in all directions but in which there was an arena surrounded by an insurmountable wall. Over this floated shouts and cheers provoked by an Olympiad from which I keenly felt my exclusion both as spectator and player. In England this perpetual tournament has no name; Americans call it 'the big time'.

These games are incapable of sharper definition than this because their rules are rearranged by each person who goes on to the field and the rewards of victory are not entirely measurable – not wholly of this world.

If you beat your head against this high wall or, indeed, against any wall, after a while it will crumble but such a course of action requires at least a positive temperament. This, if I ever had it, I lost in childhood. At a time when my two brothers aspired to be splendid icons of manliness such as firemen or ships' captains, all I wanted was to be a chronic invalid. For this vocation I had a certain flair. Unfortunately my parents decided that, as a career, it would prove too expensive. Now I could obtain a grant but then I was forced to strike out of my heart all hope of becoming a kinky Mrs Browning. Even so, nothing that has happened to me since that unhappy time has been the result of healthy, vigorous action on my part. I have always proceeded cautiously. However, even if you only lean limply against a wall and you happen to live a very long time, gradually it will begin to give way.

In my case, this process took more than half a century.

My journey from the outer suburbs almost to the heart of the city of happiness came about only partly as a result of my own feeble persistence. It was chiefly caused by a fragile chain of lucky events and by the inexplicable kindness of a series of people who knew me only slightly and one another not at all.

This entire volume is an extension of that list of acknowledgements that in other books occupies but a single paragraph.

One

By the time this century had reached its middle
sixties and I had attained my middle fifties, the
wages of art school models had risen so steeply that
the difficulty they presented was no longer how to
live on them, it had become how to deserve them.
In trying to solve this problem, the students were
little help. Nothing could persuade them to
suggest some difficult, dangerous pose that might
rouse them from their permanent lethargy. To
them life drawing was merely an arduous chore in
which there was no money; they clearly wished I
was not there.

One day when I was working in Loughton
College of Further Education, the 'life' master was
able to prevent only one of his pupils from
escaping. 'Well,' he exclaimed, turning towards her
and beaming broadly, 'the entire day, the whole
room and all of Mr Crisp are yours.' Folding her
arms across her sullen breasts, the girl replied with
the weary question, 'Why is it always up to me?'

In some ways the decline in popularity of life
drawing was a secret blessing. My physical stamina
was declining so drastically that, even if en-

thusiasm for my efforts had been evinced, I could no longer have sustained wildly heroic poses all day and every day. To conceal this fact I took to posing intermittently. In the end this would have made my declining years extremely impecunious but, for a while, I preferred this way of life; it allowed me more spare time which I put to good use by indulging in my only hobby – doing nothing.

For this innocent pastime I have always been severely criticized. When I was a child, my mother and my sister used to sit each side of a threadbare fire busily sewing or writing letters. I lay motionless on the hearth rug between them. At least once an hour one of them, with an irritable sigh, would ask, 'Why don't you get something to do?' I always replied, 'Why should I?'

Later in life, when strangers asked me what I did with my spare time and I told them I did nothing, they too instantly became agitated. To them even the most fatuous alternatives to idleness seemed preferable.

'But you don't really do nothing, do you?'

'Yes.'

'But you read.'

'Books are for writing, not for reading.'

'Well then, you write.'

'Not if I can possibly get out of it.'

'Don't you listen to the radio?'

'Listening to the radio is like holding a conversation with someone who is wearing dark glasses.'

'Then you watch television.'

'Seldom and never to kill time.'

'But you can't just do NOTHING.'

With my back to the wall I concede that I breathe and I blink. At this point my inquisitor's fury usually explodes over me like a hand grenade.

I can't deny that secretly my pathological indolence had begun to cause even me a little anxiety. I was faced with the problem which will continue to confront all elderly people until such time as the government undertakes to decide when its senior citizens shall die. The night was coming and I increasingly felt the need for a tin box full of coins lurking under the bed but, at the same time, my earning capacity was on the wane. Not only my physical strength but my resourcefulness and my optimism were gone.

By now it was years since I had applied anywhere for a specific job and decades since I had written anything and sent it unsolicited to an editor. My efforts to deal with my predicament were generalized: I leaned permanently forward so that fate could see me and I tried never to say no to anything. My chief weakness was my life-long lack of specific ambition. If a man demands a lot from fate, he will probably receive something; if he wants but little, he will almost certainly get nothing. In the long run, in spite of everything, I have been very lucky. I asked for bread and was given a stone. It turned out to be precious.

Two

One afternoon, wrapped in a filthy dressing gown and seated by my asthmatic gas fire, I was staring aimlessly at my feet which were sitting in the chair opposite me when the front door bell rang. No one was expected but I took this sign from the outer world calmly. By this time I had lived in the same room so long that I knew perhaps a hundred and fifty people any of whom might call on me without warning. On this occasion my visitor was Mr O'Connor. This I did find mildly surprising because I had not seen him for about fifteen years.

In the happy far-off time when I knew him best, Philip O'Connor was a full-time hooligan. He sat all day in layabout cafés and stood half the night in the public houses of Fitzrovia spouting improvised doggerel to friends and strangers alike without hoping or even wishing to be understood. That stage of his development was evidently past. Looking back on this incident I think he must by now have written *The Memoirs of a Public Baby* and that the instant fame that this book had brought him had introduced him to the BBC's Third

Programme. He now worked for it. This had changed him

He looked the same as before. Disraeli ringlets still hung over a brow not merely pallid but incandescent with moral decay. His eyes were still as bright as those of a sex maniac and his smile as mirthless as the hilarity of a skull. It was his personality that was different. He now wanted to get things done – an ambition absolutely forbidden in the southern confines of Bohemia which he used to frequent.

After feverishly walking up and down my room for a while, he suddenly asked if he might bring in his tape recorder. When I gave permission, he rushed downstairs returning a minute later with a contraption as big as a gas meter. (It must have been in his car – another sign of redemption from hooliganism.) As soon as he was sure that the black magic box was working, he thrust a microphone towards my astonished lips and said, 'Say something about life and death.' If I am ever told that this method of conducting an interview succeeds with other people I shall be amazed. It suited me perfectly. Compensating for the breadth of the subject by the shallowness of my views, I spoke and I spoke and I spoke. Only when the machine seemed out of breath did I stop. Mr O'Connor appeared satisfied with what had been said and left almost immediately.

I set little store by this episode. In the good old days Charlotte Street was full of people who were nearly on the stage or were just about to write a play. It seemed at the time so unlikely that anyone who had once been an habitué of that twilit land could ever in fact establish a working relationship with the real world or even with the BBC. I was wrong.

Mr O'Connor returned to my room a few days later with his boss and, when I had added a few peroratory phrases, my contribution to the programme was considered complete.

I never heard what I had said to the world because I do not listen to radio broadcasts. I cannot even say if my words were generally well received but I know that at least one person listened because, long after the entire incident was closed, I was told that a publisher had said that I ought to write a book. One's acquaintances are forever saying this even if one only makes one joke a year. The words are intended as a vague compliment rather than as specific encouragement but, if anyone in the book trade makes the remark, it must be taken seriously. Secretly I was annoyed that I had not been told of this comment sooner.

The publisher in question was called William Kimber. I was informed that he published any number of books by disused colonels and the memoirs of a lot of extinct district nurses. We had never met but I made so bold as to telephone him. He bravely admitted that the words he was rumoured to have uttered had indeed fallen from his unguarded lips. Furthermore, he promised that, if I would write a two-thousand-word synopsis of my autobiography, he would read it (or possibly cause it to be read). He would then tell me whether or not he could offer me a contract.

Even a little of my life proved too much for Mr Kimber. He wrote me a very courteous letter praising my frankness but added that he feared that, if he published a book founded on the incidents I had described, he would be bombarded from all directions with libel suits. I cannot imagine why he thought this. Though I am relentlessly outspoken about myself, I am unlikely to be indiscreet concerning others. Indeed, I seldom mention them. In any case, if I were to say that, on some specific occasion, I had popped into a dark corner with the Duke of Birmingham, a compositor could easily have set the name as 'B.rm.ngh.m' and kept the reader guessing.

I had expected Mr Kimber's reaction but being accustomed to sorrow is not the same as suffering in silence.

Late in my career as a model, I began to find the competition for employment in the London schools too fierce. I took to working in the home counties. There the college to which I went most frequently was Maidstone. I travelled thither in a railway carriage stuffed to the brim with art masters.

To them I told my tale of woe. Nothing shortens a journey so pleasantly as an account of misfortunes at which the hearer is permitted to laugh. One member of my audience was a man who, I am told, now rules Maidstone but who was then only a hireling. Even so he wielded considerable power being married to Thames and Hudson. 'Kimber!' he exclaimed, when I had come to the end of my story 'I think you can do better than that. I have my spies,' he added, 'and I will put them out.' He must have done so at once. Within a few days I was introduced to my first literary agent, a Catholic Texan married to a Protestant Irishwoman living in Putney. He submitted what I had written for Mr Kimber, together with photographs taken of me some thirty years earlier, to Messrs Jonathan Cape and in no time at all I was given a contract and £100.

I nearly fainted.

By the time the book came out I had received, I think, about £300. After that, on the English hardback edition, my royalties never amounted to much. I imagine that, when advance payments to authors are being fixed, the publisher's accountants go into a dim corner of the office, their fingers tap their thumbs rapidly and their pale lips move as they calculate exactly what the writer's earnings will be on the edition they intend to print. This is the sum offered.

I had wanted my autobiography to be called *My Reign in Hell*. I was convinced that, after turning the first few pages, readers would agree that I had closely followed Mr Lucifer's example by refusing to serve in Heaven (respectable society). This title was rejected and, from a few random ideas, *The Naked Civil Servant* was chosen. The name was suggested by an incident described towards the end of the book. A feature writer contributing to a paper called *The Scotsman* came to interview me. During our conversation or rather my monologue, while I was drawing breath he managed to ask if I was a famous model. I explained that, by that time, there was no such thing. The relationship between artists and their models had ceased to be a cause of prurient speculation not because newspapers and their readers had become any more clean-minded but for the simpler reason that painters no longer worked from the nude. Models now work only in the schools, they are engaged by the term and their wages ultimately come from the Minister of Education. They are just like civil servants except that during office hours they wear no clothes.

This title was a mistake. Almost everywhere I go, audiences ask me to explain it and, if I do not, bewilderment in the minds of book buyers gives place to fatal misunderstanding.

A friend told me that, while she was visiting her mother in Lewes, the first object that caught her eye as she entered the chintzy living-room was my book lying on a table. 'Whatever made you get that?' my friend gasped. In a calm, slightly supercilious tone her mother replied, 'I don't know what you're making such a fuss about; you know I've always been interested in the civil service.'

Before my autobiography was published I had written three books on various subjects and one longer work of fiction called *Love Made Easy*. This had been rejected – rightly as it later transpired. When, twenty-five years after it was completed, it was very kindly published by Duckworth it received bad notices even in New Zealand.

The difference between all these previous efforts to earn a living by writing and my life story was its scandal value.

The young, led to victory by the Beatles, had inherited the earth about ten years before my book was ready for publication. Their wealth has given teenagers throughout the world the power to set fashions not only in what to wear and how to dance but also in what to say. Since children always wish to talk about what their parents never mention, sex became a subject of open, nay, incessant discussion. When inevitably as a theme for table talk heterosexuality was worn threadbare, it was supplanted by homosexuality which became all the rage. The fact that the laws concerning it were in process of being changed gave this particular pastime an added topicality.

If to be a man of destiny is to arrive at a point in history when the only gift you have to offer has suddenly become relevant, then in this tiny and purely social way that is what for the moment I became.

When my book was as nearly complete as I could make it, my publisher gave me the hand of an editress in literary marriage. She was a beautiful woman whose eyes, whether she was redeeming my ungainly prose or merely shopping in Fulham Road, forever held an expression of dismayed surprise. Naturally I cannot say if she wore this look before she encountered me. She was infinitely patient, never making the slightest emendation to my typescript without consulting me, always explaining why an alteration would be for the better. If I interpret her correctly, she was advising me to make my sentences short. She was saying that, if they were in the right order, conjunctions would seldom be necessary. Then, on the rare occasion when a connecting word was used, it would be endowed with a special dramatic power of its own. I do not mean that she told me all this at any one meeting. It is what I deduce from the nature of the improvements that she urged me to make. Some years later I told her that I now write by the Miller method. I think she said, 'Come off it,' which no editress should ever say. If she happens to read this book and finds it to be full of grammatical errors no doubt her look of dismay will be intensified.

In spite of all the care lavished upon my book, it could not be described as a wild success. The reviews of it were at best kind; at worst they were, as I am sure most authors find, contradictory. One said that it was full of self-pity; someone else remarked upon its freedom from precisely this emotion. One critic was delighted by the aphorisms with which the pages were riddled; the *Times Literary Supplement* deplored the arch and jaunty style in which the story was told.

I never reject criticism on the fatuous grounds that it is prompted by unworthy motives or that to care about it is in some way beneath me. I hold that the very purpose of existence is to reconcile the glowing opinion we hold of ourselves with the appalling things that other people think about us. This book is therefore written in a minimum risk style with which I hope to offend nobody. I am aware that this does not guarantee that I shall please everybody.

Ultimately I believe that, with a hideous struggle, the hardback edition of *The Naked Civil Servant* sold out its edition of about three thousand, five hundred copies. The failure or success of the book was, however, not the point. What mattered was that another chunk of the wall against which I had for so long been leaning had given way.

Through the aperture thus created, I could now see a tantalizing corner of the arena that I longed to enter.

About a month after my autobiography was published, I was interviewed on television for the first time.

Three

To celebrate the fact that, in a parochial way, an inhabitant of the kingdom of Bohemia was beginning to make good, a hooligans' party was given. The idea for this feast was put forward by someone who during the war had himself been an habitué of the Charlotte Street cafés but who was now redeemed, firstly by marriage and secondly by having become a barrister. The arrangements for this occasion were thrust into the astonished hands of a young woman who though known to both of us had never truly been a hooliganette. It was a thoroughly embarrassing assignment that she had been given because all the guests had to be asked for money – ten shillings, I think. She implored me to supply her with a list of subscribers but I could think of no one that I would have the nerve to suggest should pay for the mere privilege of eating with me. In spite of my lack of co-operation she managed by charm and persistence to muster enough diners to enable her to hire what the Bible would call an upper room. It was in Schmidt's restaurant. Though this establishment was in the middle of Charlotte Street it presented to the world a face so cold and, worse, so clean that I do not think any of my friends had ever ventured into it before.

The party was a lively but rather awkward gathering of people whom I knew intimately, slightly or not at all. Among them was a man well-dressed and well-behaved beyond the demands of the situation. When he left the other guests asked one another in awe-struck tones, 'Who was the visitor from the outer world?'

In fact he was a televisionary who, on leaving, promised to 'see what he could do for me'. A few weeks later it was at his command that I was summoned at the dead of night to the BBC studios in Shepherd's Bush.

I found myself in the cast of a programme called *Late Night Line-Up* whose other members were a monk and Fanny Craddock. I took to her immediately because of the degree of animation that she infuses into her public appearances and, indeed, into her entire life. After the show was over and we were all sitting in the drinking room waiting for taxis to take us home, someone approached her and said, 'It's over, Fanny. It's finished.' She laughed. She had been speaking just as fast and as vigorously as when the cameras were watching her. Eagerness to please devoid of sycophancy is a characteristic I greatly admire.

While I was waiting to go into the cage with the interviewer, I was questioned three times as to whether or not I was nervous. After twice saying no I asked, 'What have I got to lose?' 'Quite right,' said my interrogator. 'Just the right attitude ' If I had been afraid, the repeated question would have turned me into a nervous wreck.

At this first interview the words 'What have I got to lose?' were uttered almost in self-defence but they exactly expressed my attitude towards the occasion. I had only negative goals. I wanted not to start every sentence with 'Well' or 'Er'. I wished to survive whatever was said to me without displaying embarrassment or shock. I need not have worried. The questions were very bland. Most of them concerned the oddities of my appearance and of my domestic routine.

As the years have flown by, the questions have remained much the same. It is the answers that have changed, not in content but in manner. I no longer regard television interviews as ordeals that must be endured without flinching. They have become welcome opportunities for presenting myself and my ideas to the world – mini-parties which I enjoy and through which I try to offer entertainment to others. I could almost say that they have become a way of life.

Within weeks of the publication of *The Naked Civil Servant* I found myself being asked to speak to small gatherings of people. They were of various denominations. Sometimes they were literary aspirants. To these I repeated that books are for writing – not for reading. To be more explicit I explained that no one who intends to take up writing as a career should read any work that lies in the category in which his own efforts would be placed. If he disobeys this rule, he will almost certainly feel that he must write literature instead of trying to say what he means. Even though he may not attempt patches of deathless prose, he will become preoccupied with grammar and syntax far more complicated than he would ever use when speaking. This is now quite unnecessary. Since the invention of Frank Norman, writing has at last ceased to be a middle-class accomplishment. It has become an activity as universal as sex and almost as exhausting.

When not with embryonic authors, I was invited to universities or art schools. There I explained that education is a mistake. Cluttering one's skull with facts about any subject other than oneself I hold to be a waste of time. All general knowledge can be discovered in the nearest public library and even these hushed and apparently harmless establishments should be visited with caution. Being well-informed is but a stone's throw from being boring and stones will be thrown.

In seats of learning on whatever social level audiences are often livelier than elsewhere. While I was talking to the inmates of East Ham Polytechnic one young man abruptly stumbled out of the room. He returned a few minutes later with the explanation that he had found it prudent to stand in the corridor for a while to cool his rage. 'You're lucky,' he warned me, 'I've got a terrible temper and I nearly clobbered you.' What had so incensed him was my statement that artists should disregard social issues. East Ham is a fully committed region.

Inevitably the audiences that I was most often asked to amuse were members of the Campaign for

Homosexual Equality or other kindred organizations. If I spoke to Lesbian societies, no men were ever present. Perhaps like a masonic lodge in reverse they occasionally held a gentlemen's night but I never attended one. Their policy at that time seemed to be gently isolationist. To give an example: at a mixed gathering in Croydon, a girl said, 'I suppose I shouldn't ask you this but why do the boys keep on at us to come to their meetings? I can't see any point.' I gave a non-committal reply to conceal my surprise at this question. Traditionally, in the heterosexual world, it is the men who will not attend any social occasion unless it holds carnal possibilities. That is what makes them so hard to get along with. I was sorry to be made aware that girls were now adopting this bleak way of thinking.

As the years went by, matters worsened. Lesbian attitudes towards gay men passed from indifference to hostility and upon any manifestation of effeminacy they began to pour open contempt. It was regarded not so much as sinful or repulsive as politically ineffectual. One of the surest ways of making yourself and other people notice your masculinity (whether you are in fact a man or not) is to talk incessantly about politics or money. This is what the majority of Lesbians had decided to do. Their 'cause' became almost synonymous with Women's Liberation. The partial merging of these two factions was almost inevitable. Not many liberationists would say that they demanded the right to make love with partners of whatever sex they chose but many Lesbians would certainly state that they wished for a life in which they could enter without question all masculine territory including that of sharing and possibly shouldering the financial burdens of living with a woman. There is on the other hand a species of gay man which finds the practical worries of life intimidating. Such a person likes the society of girls because he hopes that with them conversation will be less worldly, less political, less mercenary. For this reason there were usually a few women at gatherings arranged by male homosexuals. Their presence made functions look well attended and their subscriptions swelled party funds. None of the boys seemed threatened by them.

If I were asked to describe the difference between the sexes in the gay world, I would say that the men wanted to be amused; the girls sought vindication.

In the late sixties it seemed to me that these meetings were mostly genuinely social. If they were political, they were not stridently so. If, secretly, they were vast shopping centres, they never exuded that atmosphere both crude and furtive which makes frequenting gay public houses such a daunting prospect.

Once, while I was in Bristol helping to declare it a gay city, the convener of the event said, 'This is gay week – and I mean GAY. I know that the place is full of gay bars and that many of you stand in them night after night but you never speak to anyone, you never seem to be enjoying yourselves.' That young man had all my sympathy.

From the beginning, the Campaign for Homosexual Equality was as fundamentally political as the word 'campaign' implies but it also catered for the human needs of its members. Trips along the Thames, musical evenings, even a CHE fair were arranged. Perhaps because my sister was the wife of a country parson, I was quite accustomed to such activities and I was never contemptuous of their parochial element. I was also aware that, if there had been such an organization when I was young, I would have been a founder member. If there had been in existence any building in London where the very thing that made it impossible for me to feel at ease with other groups of men would have been taken for granted, I would have been on the doorstep before the place was opened.

In the early days, whether speaking to men, women or a mixture of the two, I always assumed that my function was to entertain but I did occasionally issue warnings. One of these was against forming an exile's view of reality. It was, I thought, likely to be as wide of the mark as Mr Browning's idea of an English April. Just because full-time homosexuals are on the outside of certain experiences — just because they stand with their cold noses pressed against the window pane gazing through it at the carpet-slipper set-up — they should not suppose that everything by the fireside is permanent, peaceful. The terrible truth is that the people on the inside are trying to get out.

At all these events I was indulgently received and very courteously treated. Someone always fetched me, fed me and transported me back to Beaufort Street when the evening ended. The Campaign was poor and so was I. A fee of about £5 was most acceptable and these transactions had about them a pleasant amateurishness. Inevitably, as my hold on the reins of my band-wagon tightened, this passed.

I am writing of a time when I was both working as a model and giving these small talks. Between them these two professions earned me a living but I was aware that I ought to be turning my new situation to better account. I was still not in the arena – not even in a ringside seat. All my friends tried to help but no fringe benefits seemed to dangle from the fact of my having written a book. My agent came to the rescue.

He was not content with trafficking in the work of others, he also wished to write. Like a nurse ministering to the sick in a plague of words, it was only to be expected that eventually he himself would succumb to the disease. The theme that he chose as the subject for his own book was style – not of writing but of living. He showed me a list of chapter headings, a plan of campaign and so on and asked me what I thought of them. I replied that they displayed masterly powers of organization but added that, as a way of convincing a publisher that a book was actually in the process of being written, they were a dead loss. I suggested that what was needed was a tin suitcase stuffed to bursting with typescript. My agent agreed and solicited my help. The longer I contemplated the subject he had selected, the more opinions I found

I had. I wrote and I wrote and I wrote. When the gold – well, the yellow metal – was sifted from the dross of my discourse, there appeared to be very little that would enrich the publisher to whom it was to be presented. Though I was most hand-somely rewarded for my useless assistance, I felt somehow let down. I had the nerve to borrow back the work for which I had already been paid and take it to Messrs Jonathan Cape whence it was returned as quickly as if we had been playing badminton. I embraced my oldest friend defeat and went on as though nothing unpleasant had happened. My agent fled to Texas.

My unloved typescript lay among the fluff under my bed until I received a visit from an actress who had divorced the stage and married a member of the legendary Woolf family. As she reclined amidst the dust of my room, she asked wistfully, 'Don't you ever write anything that Cecil could publish?'

I dived under the bed and brought out my thoughts on style, now a greyish-yellow in colour. 'If he doesn't want them,' I said with a bitter laugh, 'throw them away.' This statement I later regret-ted. When I asked for the return of my work, I inadvertently brought into effect Proust's First Law. Love does not cause jealousy; it is jealousy that engenders love. The moment it was implied that I had found a use for my typescript, Mr Woolf's indifference vanished. He decided to publish a book on style.

The recall of my literary effort was not a ruse. I wanted it because I thought it might be of interest to Mr Mitchell, the famous maker of television documentaries.

Looked at from the front, a television screen is a small space in which personalities and events jostle one another for a brief moment of glory or, at least, of public attention. Seen from behind it is an arid waste in which, like farmers in a dust bowl, broadcasters and producers dig for something – anything – on which to feed their bleating flocks. If somewhere there is a woman who has made the largest patchwork quilt in the world, immediately this is known documentary interest in her will become keen – nay, desperate. 'Get her,' snarls the director. 'She's in the Antarctic,' his secretary quietly explains. 'Get her,' her employer repeats louder than before. The indefatigable needlewoman is snatched by helicopter from the ice floes, her air fare to New York is paid, she is placed in an expensive hotel. The next day she murmurs a few shy words into a microphone and is returned to the everlasting snows. Only God and Mr Bernstein know the cost of such an escapade.

When not even this much material is to hand, a programme is made about Soho.

For this reason I was not altogether surprised when, walking innocently along Old Compton Street, I was waylaid by an acquaintance with the question, 'Do you want to be in a thing about Soho?'

'Another?'

'Yes, another.'

I remembered with how little enthusiasm I had occasionally watched these programmes. They are invariably mixtures of interviews with bemused Italian caterers, insults from beery Bohemians and the confessions of bored prostitutes. Even so, I nodded. If we wish to be totally free from blame for our anonymity, we must never say no to anything.

So much later that I had quite forgotten the few words exchanged in the street, a minor tele-visionary whom I had never met telephoned me to remind me of them. I agreed to meet him in the As-You-Like-It Coffee Bar in Monmouth Street. This was positively the last of the layabout cafés – those marvellous places where you could sit through lunch and tea and supper without ordering anything more than one cup of coffee. I chose this venue so that, if the appointment was not kept, it would not in any way disturb my way of life. It was an establishment where several times a week, either accompanied or alone, I sat for hours eating lotus petals.

As it happened I was not betrayed. The stranger fed me with tea and questions about the difference between Soho now and what it had been like when I was young. I explained that the district had gone down terribly. You used to be able to get your throat cut on a really big scale but now the entire region was riddled with nothing better than dim basements where girls take off their clothes for money. I pointed out that, as a test of the closeness of your relationship with the world, sex could never be a patch on being murdered. (That's when someone really does risk his life for you.) My inquisitor seemed dazed rather than enlightened by what I said but he must have regaled his employers with a favourable account of our meeting because, after another interval of several weeks, he telephoned me again.

This time he wished me to go immediately to a public house in Greek Street. There, half an hour later, I found the televisionary, two members of a pop group called The Strawbs and Mr Mitchell whose genius for television documentaries was explained to me. He wore a suit and seemed slightly ill at ease. To offset this, he was very friendly and bought innumerable drinks for all of us. At that time I formed no positive opinion of him whatsoever. This I later learned is the minimal impression that he aims to create at all times. He was the first to leave the party saying, 'We must meet again some time,' which everyone knows is English for good-bye. I was therefore astonished when, within a few days, he visited my room in Chelsea. During the next few weeks several conversations between us took place either at my home or his which was temporarily in London. To me our discussions did not seem particularly purposeful but they must have been to him for a day finally came when he said, 'I think we'll make it all in this room.'

'Make what?' I asked.

'The film.'

'About Soho?'

'It won't be about Soho.'

'Then what will it be about?'

'You.'

Early in October of 1968 a production team of

six marched on Beaufort Street. So small is my room that the sound equipment and the two men who claimed to understand it were compelled to spend all their working hours in the bathroom. The girl who lived in the back room on my floor couldn't go to the gent's for a week. Not only was the routine of the house disrupted, the whole street was disturbed by a generator which chugged away happily outside the front door until the neighbours complained. Sheets of pink acetate were fixed over the windows of my room and for four days as though lit by the dawn of a new Doris day, I walked about, sat in my chair or rolled on my bed droning on about eternal things. The resulting abundance of material I am happy to tell you was rendered down until it lasted only half an hour and was shown on Granada Television at the end of the following year. This programme was well received except by the *Daily Express* and even that paper savaged me rather than the makers of the film.

The public curiosity aroused caused an unknown woman working for Granada to telephone me.

'They keep asking who you are,' she complained.

'Who indeed?' said I.

'Apparently there's some book that you've written.'

I admitted that I was the author of a meagre number of books and mentioned that the latest of these was called *The Naked Civil Servant*. She seemed content with this information and I heard

35

no more from her. Evidently, as far as she was concerned, the mystery was solved. For me it merely deepened.

I had no difficulty in understanding why, from the television company's point of view, no mention of the book must be made during the programme. Had it been, the entire project might then have seemed to be an advertisement for which the wrong people were being paid. Worse, my ingrained eccentricities might have appeared to be assumed for the purpose of boosting book sales. What I found strange was that, when the papers mentioned the time at which the documentary was being shown, they made no reference to the book, and in no advertisement for the book was anything said to connect me with the film. My bewilderment mounted to downright astonishment when I learned that the publishing house and the television company concerned were as one on this matter.

You cannot turn your toes towards Golden Square without being asked of any programme you have made, 'Will it be part of a series?' I have no idea whether Mr Mitchell was asked to make other films similar to mine after it turned out to be a mild success or whether, before he began, he already thought of it as one of several such features. The final result was that the film about me was shown twice, first by itself and later as the first of six documentaries about old men looking back on their lives.

After all these events I came to know the Mitchells personally. They proposed that another film should be made, this time not about my habits but my opinions. It was to help with this project that I asked Mr Woolf to return my book about style.

When this second documentary did not materialize I was disappointed. It seemed that fate had thrust me back into limbo or, at least, not drawn me forward. I did not dream that one day, beautifully made though it was, Mr Mitchell's film, in terms of publicity, would seem no more than a trailer for the television version of *The Naked Civil Servant*.

I still hold Mr and Mrs Mitchell in the highest regard and we write to each other at Christmas time but it has become doubtful that we will ever make another television programme together. In a small way I now live the 'show biz' life which to Mr Mitchell is like cock-crow to a vampire. The word 'actor' causes him to fling his arm across his eyes and fall back against the nearest wall.

Four

Immediately after the publication of my auto-biography in 1968, I had begun to receive telephone calls from part or total strangers at the rate of one a week and about twice as many letters. When I asked a friend if she had ever written to anyone she didn't know, she replied, 'Of course I have. You're far more likely to find you have something in common with someone whose work you admire than with a man who merely happens to have married your sister.' I bowed my head before the invincible logic of this observation but I have never corresponded with a total stranger in all my long, dark life. I wouldn't dare. This may be why I regarded the communications I received with such amazement.

I once said that I liked my friends but that I was simply mad about strangers. This is still true but during the past twelve years my attitude towards people whom I do not know has changed. If possible, their reaction to me has become even more extreme and, consequently, mine to them has grown more cautious. The letters that now rained down upon me usually came from women. This was natural enough. Men say they have no time to write letters but they rise at dawn to jog, watch television until midnight and even neglect their own best interests to pursue activities they enjoy. We must therefore conclude that they do not like correspondence that does not begin 'Your esteemed favour to hand . . .' While at that time the spoken messages to me were polite, interested, amused, the written ones were often sad. They began, 'You won't remember me but . . .' or 'You don't know me but . . .' These words were preceded by a few kind phrases of eulogy about my life or my book – payment in advance for the sympathy about to be solicited.

What followed was usually a vague cry for help. The burden that was too great to bear was life itself – a feeling that, from my youth, I understood so well. My attention was being engaged not because it was thought that I possessed any specific knowledge but because it was known that I would never be shocked or bored or feel tempted to tell anyone to pull herself together. On the few occasions when these appeals came to me not by post but through the telephone, I realized that my main function was to listen.

I hold that words are the salve with which we heal the wounds inflicted on us by our actions. If an unpleasant incident is described often enough, its sharp edges become bevelled. Moreover, if a problem is stated with sufficient accuracy, the solution has already been formulated. I merely waited, almost in silence, for this to happen. Occasionally strangers asked me for practical advice: 'Shall I leave my husband?' or 'Shall I tell my parents that I'm gay?' The first remedy that I suggested was to do nothing. To young men who felt that their homosexuality was a social handicap, I recommended that they should neither confirm nor deny it. If asked to amplify this statement, I said, 'Don't become involved in a dialogue which might lead anyone to suppose that you are likely to marry someone of the opposite sex with whom you have been to the movies twice; on the other hand there is no need to waltz down to breakfast with the words "Guess what?"'

Unfortunately I have found no way of keeping out of these exchanges, whether written or spoken, an element of condescension. A grandparent-grandchild relationship, that is not entirely due to my age, inevitably sets in.

Since leaving home I have never had any problems other than financial. I have not been deeply involved with anyone. In the house where to this day I have a room, there once lived a woman whose lust for rows and reconciliations to some extent involved the lives of all the inmates. When we realized that her recantations were nothing but a means of not paying the usual price for speaking one's mind, we came to despise her apologies more than her rages. Even I did not quite succeed in avoiding either but I tried. My desire was never to win this woman's good opinion but always to have a quiet life. When threatened, my wish is to disengage myself – so that not even a fragment of my life resides in someone else's. Therefore, when anyone presents me with human problems, I have no similar experience to offer in exchange. If any of my unknown correspondents has felt deflated by this, I here ask forgiveness. It would be heartless to say that I enjoy hearing about the misfortunes of others but it is true that I profit by becoming acquainted with them. It brings me a little nearer to understanding people. If they are grateful for my sympathy, I am glad of their confidence.

These encounters of the fourth kind were just beginning to abate when Mr Mitchell's documentary about me was shown on Granada Television. After it, the letters continued their gradual decline in numbers but the telephone calls became more frequent and their character became more hostile, or perhaps it would be truer to say they became more contemptuous. Evidently letter-writers are a restrained race while televiewers are a violent people.

I imagine that the nuisance calls came chiefly from girls working on switchboards. Such conversations would be useless without an audience who could hear both ends. Besides, it was often possible to detect a certain hollowness not only in the content of these dialogues but also in their sound and, once in a while, another voice than that of the original caller would interrupt a long silence with the question, 'Is he still on the line?' When this happened, I replied that I was, but suggested that, as none of us had come up with anything very witty, it might be as well to ring off.

Some calls sought merely to inconvenience me. A girl would pose as an employee of some well-known television company and would ask me to go, say, to Euston Station to be photographed. I replied that she must communicate with my agent.

'We don't work through agents.'

'Then I fear that we cannot come to a satisfactory arrangement.'

'We'll make it worth your while.'

'You're very kind.'

'Then will you do it?'

'No.'

At other times an effort was made to embarrass me socially. A young woman would say that she was giving a party. I would wish her every success.

'Will you come?'

'No, thank you.'

'There will be lots of lovely boys.'

'How nice!'

'Then won't you come?'

'No, thank you.'

This kind of discourse frequently continued for several minutes.

I could have understood these feeble attempts at entrapment if the programme that provoked them had left my homosexuality vague. If a viewer merely suspected my guilty secret, she might regard it as a triumph of perspicacity if she could trick me into giving some sign that her suspicions were correct. As my sin was never in any doubt, what could anyone gain even if I expressed ludicrous eagerness to attend a kinky orgy?

I have often been asked why I am so patient with these unseen enemies. The cause is partly habit. I was the youngest child and consequently was the butt of mockery and abuse almost from birth. The

43

only member of my family who did not heap ridicule upon me was my father and that was because he never spoke. I would have died of exhaustion if I had tried to combat the treatment I received; instead I feigned not to be angry. The only method known to me by which one can survive one's emotions is to feign not to have them.

It works. I am now almost entirely free from indignation. I can't remember the last time I 'answered back'.

Other-cheekism is not only a way of purifying the soul, it is also part of every weak person's survival kit. If I had tried to defend myself in any of the street incidents of which in my youth I was the victim, I might easily have been killed. I seem now to be in less physical danger than formerly but even when dealing with verbal harassment the principle is the same. If, as soon as the hostility of a stranger reaches me through the telephone, I were to put the receiver back on its cradle, my tormentor would ring again and again. If I shouted at him, he would goad me with redoubled savagery.

I also remind myself that if I, however gently, have insisted on preserving my personal freedom I must never try to curtail the liberty of others – even when it takes the form of baiting a complete stranger.

When teasing calls came from men, they were seldom openly hostile. They tended to be pseudo-subtle. A voice like that of a monitor lizard would announce itself as Nigel or Basil or any other name thought to be slightly precious and would claim to have met me in Hyde Park or Piccadilly Circus. As I have not tried to pick anybody up for fifty years nor even made myself conspicuously available for thirty, I was always certain that these statements were a flimsy hoax. I merely declined politely whatever invitation was offered. Very occasionally these assignatory calls were genuine in the sense that, though my caller could hardly long to know me, he might wish to find out certain things about himself and might feel that in me he had found someone who, without either giggling or being contemptuous, would assist his self-knowledge.

'You're Quentin Crisp,' the voice would say.

I would reply that I was.

'You've written a book or been on a telly programme about homosexuality?'

'Ye-es.'

'Well I've never done anything like that but I've wanted to.'

'Thousands have.'

'It's a question of getting someone to do it to me [or for me or with me].'

'I'm afraid that I can't help you but I hope you find someone who will.'

Sometimes I made so bold as to suggest that Nigel or Basil sought someone nearer his own age and whom he actually liked. Here again I wanted to show that I was not disgusted. I felt mean in refusing to become involved in these proposed experiments. I hate to think that there is anyone in the world who never fulfils his fantasies because of mere shyness but I could not be sure that the situation was what it seemed. I was afraid. I am an old man of feeble physique. It would be foolish of me to place myself in a room with a stranger so odd, so obviously peculiar, that none of his friends had ever made the slightest attempt to help him overcome his self-doubt.

And how did such people think of me? Did they envisage me in rimless glasses and a white coat, standing at the top of the stairs and saying, 'Next, please'?

Sometimes I persuaded callers to pass through the social equivalent of the metal detector used at airports. I made an appointment in the not so immediate future. The introduction of a time-lag eliminated all the jokey customers and nearly all the kinky ones but once a youth kept one of these delayed assignations. He was about twenty years of age, tall, slim and with blond hair faintly gilded by artificial means. He talked for about an hour. That was how long it took to reach the subject of sadomasochism. I explained that I had been lucky – that, even in my youth when my poverty was at its bleakest, I had not been forced to take part in painful situations of the kind to which he was referring. I gave no sign that I knew we had now reached the heart of our discourse nor did he but he left soon after my disclaimer.

I was amazed that anyone so presentable had found no way of stirring into his relationships with his friends a little at a time of his favourite flavouring.

When, many years later, Mr Mackie's television play about me was shown to the world, these telephone calls passed from tittering contempt to growling hatred. For the first time direct threats upon my life were screamed at me from invisible lips: 'You're queer. I'll kill you.' I could only ask if the speaker wanted an appointment. It was not possible to take these menaces seriously. I regarded them as no more real than the offers of rape that are forever being made to girls with foreign surnames listed in English telephone books. I have no doubt that England is bristling with people sincerely longing for my death and, when they can tolerate my existence no further, presumably they will jump without warning from behind a tree in the street where I live.

It was also noticeable that, with the passage of time, harassment was starting to come from younger and younger boys. Once a schoolmaster whom I have known for many years was visiting with me. I placed him by the telephone so that he could act as a taster for the poison dripping from the ear piece. On that day we received several hostile calls in the course of a few hours. They required no replies; they were merely a spate of filthy words. My friend judged them to be from boys no more than twelve-years-old.

And why do I not have my name removed from the telephone book? I gave up being a model in the art schools in June of '78 so I can no longer claim that the telephone represents money but the answer was never as simple as that. The first objection to becoming 'ex-directory' is that it looks as though you think you are somebody. The second reason for not doing so is that it would be ages before the gesture took effect. It would be a year at least before the A-D section without my name in it was published and even then all the old copies would not instantly be swept from the face of London. Furthermore, my number would still be engraved upon the stony heart of every schoolboy in England. He will forget only when the notion of sex ceases to torment him. Finally, and more important than all other objections, is the feeling that, if your number is no longer in circulation, like Electra, you have shut the windows of your house forever. From that terrible moment onwards, you will never see the outer world again; you will be stuck with your friends.

In spite of all that my persecutors can do or say to me, I still want the world. What else is there?

The most unusual threat to my life came from a woman. She was in no way inimical. In fact killing me was to be an act of mercy.

Shortly before I departed for America the second time, I received a flattering letter from the north of England. Later the writer telephoned me to say that she was coming to London to show artwork of some kind to a prospective buyer and would like to weave into her itinerary a visit to my room. I agreed. This woman, neither old nor young, turned out to be of neat appearance and, during the entire time that she spent with me, she neither did nor said anything the least bit peculiar. Nevertheless, several days after our meeting, I found, wedged between the door of my room and its frame, a piece of paper informing me that a police inspector from the local station wished to see me urgently. Within half an hour of my telephoning him, he and one of his accomplices were in my room.

Times have changed. The last occasion on which the law had invaded my privacy occurred during the war. Since then it had never paid me a visit and had seldom questioned me in the street. I do not deny that in the past it treated me better than it might have done and this is not my opinion alone. When someone showed the teleplay of my life to a police officer, his first words were, 'Can't be true.' Asked how he was so sure of this, the man replied, 'He'd have been arrested on the first day.' I myself have often wondered why it took so long for anyone to get around to 'taking me in for questioning', considering that I used to waltz along the streets of the West End totally unaware that they were infested with plainclothes coppers. Though they did not arrest me until 1943, they knew that I was in a weak position and constantly threatened me for their own and one another's amusement. Their condescension towards me on these occasions will never fade from my mind. Even now I could never wittingly become acquainted with a policeman; nor would I, except under torture, betray anyone to the authorities. Life is so hard for poor little crooks at the best of times.

I imagine that these opinions which I hold so intensely are, in a milder form, fairly common. As a former police chief has himself said, 'If the police were popular there would be something wrong somewhere.'

On this occasion I tried to give no hint of any of

these feelings and invited the men to sit down. For their part, though they could not prevent their invasion from being sinister, their manner of questioning me was in no way aggressive.

The inspector informed me that he had that morning received a letter from my female visitor. He showed me a copy of it which had been typed out on a long strip of paper in such a way as to keep exactly the same number of words on each line as were in the original manuscript. It looked like a printer's galley for a poem by e. e. cummings and, when read aloud, it made as little sense. The writer explained who and what she was, stating also that she was a Lesbian. She described her visit to my room and her reactions to the occasion. She had apparently been overwhelmed by the spectacle of my loneliness. It was to put an end to this that she proposed to kill me and then, so as to leave no loose ends, to do away with herself.

While my visitors questioned me, I tried to think what on earth could have provoked this deeply emotional response in a total stranger. If living alone was mentioned, I am sure that I uttered no cries of anguish. It is a subject that either from the stage or on equal terms I have discussed with many people and I have always explained that I prefer to live by myself so that I may have time and space to recharge my batteries before my next onslaught upon the world. By the time I met this woman my life had in fact become unexpectedly satisfactory. I doubt that I complained about anything.

I suggested to the police that they should ignore the letter as I intended to do. This they said would be improper. I had no idea that I was making an improper suggestion to a constable. It seems that for one human being to threaten the life of another is an offence. It is only because such menaces are usually delivered verbally leaving behind no usable evidence that cases of this nature seldom come to court. The inspector told me that he felt compelled to communicate the following day with the constabulary in the town where the letter-writer lived. I made no effort to dissuade him from doing this. It was obviously what the woman most desired in life, otherwise she would have carried out her bizzare plan without any advance publicity. Perhaps she was kinky for policewomen. What happened to her I have no idea.

Now that England has become so easy to live in, now that no one who resides here need work or suffer any other curtailment of liberty, it is difficult not to despise someone who goes to such lengths as I have just described in order to draw attention to herself. The ruse seemed specially obnoxious in that it involved someone else (for whom, incidentally, sycophantic admiration had been expressed) in the degrading experience of a visit from the police. Yet even an incident as unpleasant as this was not a total loss; it shed a murky ray of light on a particular area of human experience.

If male homosexuality is, as some people seem to think, a way of enjoying sex without the unpleasantness of involvement, then may not Lesbianism be the opposite, may it not spring from a dread of emotional isolation? Certain women may, almost from birth, be made aware by their home life that companionship between the sexes is, to say the least, unlikely. This realization could cause them to gravitate towards the exclusively feminine world where, if a girl is lucky, she may find a partner who is willing, even eager, to spend twenty-four hours a day with her – someone who will sit on the edge of the bath and watch her washing her hair. Though I am now over seventy, I still receive messages, sent in the kindest spirit, willing on me the horrors of eternal love. These friendly wishes always come from Lesbians. Sometimes I ask one of these women how she imagines I could remain wise, witty and beautiful from dawn till dusk and beyond. She never tells me. My question, which is absolutely sincere, is evaded by the use of platitudes. It is explained that all relationships require a little give and take. This is untrue. Any partnership demands that we give and give and give and at the last, as we flop into our graves exhausted, we are told that we didn't give enough. Everyone knows this but so great was my prospective murderess's fear of isolation that she could not conceive of my living alone as a way of being content.

Occasionally mysterious telephone calls have been intended to seduce me not into mere folly but into crime.

One evening, when the telephone bell rang and I laid my eager ear to the keyhole of the world, I heard the sound of laughter and more than one voice speaking in an unknown tongue. After a moment, this babble sorted itself out and one man with a broken or perhaps only chipped accent took over the conversation. He told me that he had just arrived in England from Norway where he claimed that the story of my life had recently been shown on television. The programme in question had not been shown there but I did not contradict him; it would not have befitted my station in life. Then a small sexless voice interrupted this dialogue to explain that its name was Jasper. Another lie, I said to myself. No one since my godfather has been called by that name and he was so unbalanced by the burden that he took to wearing a monocle.

During the next afternoon the front door bell rang. Ah, another person, I thought rubbing my hands together with glee. I was wrong. On the doorstep there was only half a person – a child of less than eight who suffered from some hideous disease which caused him to blink compulsively. Once again he announced that he was Jasper. 'Semi-precious,' I snorted. 'I knew there would be something wrong.' I looked over the child's head into the street. Slavering white-slavers were nowhere to be seen. There was no way of returning this baggage to its sender. I was dressed in nothing but socks and a dressing-gown. Pointing to these, I excused myself from inviting Jasper into the house and shut the door on him.

If this incident was a clumsy attempt at entrapment by the police, I suppose we must .ry to find it in our hearts to praise their ingenuity. If it was the work of a civilian, we are forced to conclude that Norway is full of people who, to put to some feeble test a homosexual person whom they do not know, will subject children to embarrassment, unpleasantness, terror and even the possibility of a fate worse than life.

The notion, evidently universally held in Norway and not unknown elsewhere, that all homosexuals are sexually interested in small boys, is without foundation. The number of gay men who molest or wish to molest small boys is no greater than the number of sad heterosexuals who want to interfere with little girls. Of those homosexuals who do harbour these desires, none is obvious or camp for the simple reason that only effeminate men look for liaisons in which they can indulge their helplessness, their frailty. Translated into physical terms, the deepest sexual longings of this type of man are mainly for passive sodomy and in this context the equipment of children is inadequate. My guess, but of this I admit that I have no proof, is that child molesters go to work on children of either sex with no preference whatsoever.

It may be hard to believe but glimpses of the human soul have been revealed to me even more revolting than what psychologists will one day call the Norwegian psychosis.

I once received a telephone call from a strange man who said that he held a letter with my name on the envelope but which had arrived at the house in Hampstead where my agent formerly lived.

'Are you with him now?' I asked eagerly. The thief replied that he was not. Somewhat bewildered I thanked him for telephoning me and humbly asked him to forward my property to me.

When, after about three weeks, this had not been done, I journeyed all the way to Hampstead to the house where I had so often called on my agent. As always I found the street door open and went up to the top flat. A woman came to the door with a towel wrapped round her head. I apologized for troubling her at what was obviously an inopportune moment and explained why I had called. 'Your letter's not here,' she said. 'It's in Streatham.' She offered no reason why this should be so nor did she evince any shame that she had taken it upon herself to distribute among the poor something that did not belong to her. On the other hand there was no sniggering and no hostility was manifested. She even offered to telephone the address in the deep south of London to which she had so inexplicably taken my property. Her accomplice there said that he did not have my letter – that it was in his flatmate's room.

Tentatively I asked if I might take away with me the number she had just dialled. This she gave me without hesitation. Then, holding the towel about her head, she walked down several flights of stairs with me. I found this mixture of courtesy and diabolical cruelty in her nature absolutely baffling. When we reached street level, she said, 'We opened the envelope.' Again there seemed to be no hint as to whether this statement was a boast or a confession. 'What did my correspondent say?' I asked, trying to match her calmness though by now I was in agony. The young woman could not remember in detail but she recalled that the letter had come from Greece and that it was about the possibility of translating *The Naked Civil Servant* into Greek. I now at least knew that whatever the actual message was, it came from a Mr Valamvanos who a long time ago had proposed this idea.

When I reached home, I telephoned Streatham. The missing young man had returned. He read to me what my Mediterranean friend had written. I thanked him and asked that my letter be forwarded to me. It was agreed that this should be done and, in about three weeks' time, I finally received it with a Notting Hill postmark. Like their accomplice in Hampstead, the culprits in Streatham also offered no explanation – certainly no apology.

Until this bizarre incident occurred, I would have said that there were three ways of dealing with mail which arrives in your house but is addressed to someone no longer living there. You can ignore the beastly stuff forever: you can repost it with the sad word 'Unknown' written across the envelope; or, if your life is exceptionally dull, you might try reading it and then throwing it away.

Now I know that there are other ways of coping with communications that do not belong to you. You can hand them round like chocolates among your friends.

I did not feel that the men in this case had behaved any worse than such people usually do. Their natures were obviously too complex for them simply to reseal the envelope and despatch it to my address which has been in the telephone book since before either of them was born but at least they had felt that I ought not to be altogether cut off from my friend abroad. Their delay in ultimately reposting my letter may have been due to their regarding this gesture as a mere formality. They had already acquainted me with the contents and had been patient enough to spell out to me the address from which they came.

The girl's behaviour is another matter. Many years ago, when I read *Les Liaisons Dangereuses*, it seemed to me that the antics of the principal characters were nonsense – that no one would spend all that time and ingenuity on ruining the life of another human being. When I gave utterance to this criticism, someone pointed out to me that, at the time when this book was written, the aristocracy of France had absolutely nothing with which to fill its days except a little amusing evil. I now realize that, even in the busy modern world, there are those among us who take up sadism like skate-boarding. The fact that the girl in Hampstead opened my letter meant that almost certainly she knew who I was. This being so, she must have been aware of my circumstances – that I live on the fringe of destitution. Nevertheless she deliberately withheld from me information that might have led to my receiving money for translation rights. This young woman was not ill-favoured; presumably she could have found other pleasurable ways of filling in time between now and the grave and yet she chose to weave this diabolical plot against me.

In the end, the Greek offer was not accepted. As Miss Hampstead hoped, my penury continued but for different reasons. In my opinion this in no way mitigates her sin.

I have dealt so far chiefly with the remote and the hostile communications that I have received from the outer world. There is a connection between them. It is less embarrassing, less dangerous, to abuse someone from a distance. My face-to-face encounters with strangers in recent times have improved dramatically – nay, they have reversed their nature. I have passed from being an outcast to being almost universally acceptable with such speed that I have had no time to experience ordinary life. I am never with people; they are in my presence. I never take part in conversations; I am subjected to interviews. This has happened because television is a redemptive medium. If any reader of this book is in the grip of some habit of which he is deeply ashamed, I advise him not to give way to it in secret but to do it on television No one will pass him by with averted gaze on the other side of the street. People will cross the road at the risk of losing their own lives in order to say 'We saw you on the telly.'

The Thames rendering of my life story was, quite rightly, a saga of human depravity. It offered to the viewers visual proof of what previously had only been suspected, feared or, possibly, hoped. This did indeed cause certain people to despise me even more deeply than before but in the eyes of others I gradually started to become sanctified.

Five

That my book was made into a television play was a miracle or rather a series of tiny miracles in which I played only the most passive part. These events began as far back as 1970.

While I was hard at work writing my book about life-style or sitting by the fire wishing I were hard at work, I received a message from Messrs Jonathan Cape. They wished to know if the movie rights in *The Naked Civil Servant* were for sale. I thought the question must be a joke. When told that the enquiry came from a Mr Haggarty, my amazement and amusement increased a hundred-fold. In the long chain of men and women by whose kindness I have been handed through the crowd, nearer and nearer to the front of it like someone who has fainted at the boat race, this man is the totally inexplicable link.

During the war Mr Haggarty was an airman but his feet were surprisingly often on the ground of Fitzrovia where he enjoyed the status of an honorary hooligan. He was kinky for tall girls, which took up a lot of his time but occasionally, perhaps from exhaustion, he sat at the same tables in the same cafés as the rest of us. Towards the end of the war he disappeared. Possibly he went to fight somebody. Coming down to earth again when peace broke out, he landed in the documentary film industry. While thus employed, he overtook me one day as I was walking innocently along a turning out of Wardour Street. I told him that I was writing a book which was in part about the making of short movies. 'Will it', he suggested, 'be called *Nobody Ordered Crisps?*'

Twenty years later, when I telephoned him to ask if his enquiry about my life story was serious, he assured me that it was. Into this conversation he introduced the fair name of Philip Mackie. Though I now listen eagerly to every word of his wonderful television plays, I must admit with downcast eyes and cheeks scarlet with shame that at that time I had never heard of him. He lives in Buckingham Street and, when negotiations and options and contracts and all that rubbish were settled, it was in his flat there that the three of us used to meet.

For some time we talked airily about my sex life – a subject of which I almost never tire – but in the end I could not help pausing to ask Mr Haggarty what he stood to gain from the project under discussion.

'Is Mr Mackie going to produce this movie and are you going to write it?' I asked. To my utter bewilderment the answer was no.

'I'm casting my bread upon the waters,' Mr Haggarty explained and added, 'you've heard of people doing that.'

60

Indeed, I had. For a life-time I had been standing on the river bank with a bent pin trying to fish some of it out, but to this day some of my puzzlement about Mr Haggarty remains. Years later I designed the programme cover of a play by him which was performed in a dried-up fish pond in a dim basement in Leicester Square. It hardly seemed an adequate reward to offer someone who had altered the whole course of my life.

Within four years of the televising of *The Naked Civil Servant*, I, for whom until then a journey to Ealing amounted to an awfully big adventure, had visited Canada, Australia and the United States. I had also met dozens of people so far above me in wealth, social standing and achievement that they seemed to have come from another planet. I am constantly asked if I now meet more interesting people than formerly. I never let the question pass To me everyone is interesting who will talk about himself but, when I said this in Toronto, I was laughed to scorn by one of the city's drama critics. I have therefore since then revised this statement. I now claim that everyone is interesting who will tell the truth about himself.

Although these changes were spectacular, there is a sense in which they were superficial; they altered my engagement calendar but not my soul. This was in the nature of things. Events and personalities did not begin to crowd in on me until I was sixty-six and inner development was no longer possible. Perhaps it was an outward sign of this internal stagnation that I in no way expanded my home life. I continued to live in my small, dusty room, to drink Complan and to wear other people's cast-off clothes. Even out of doors my manner changed only in that I no longer stalked through the streets scorning people before they had a chance to scorn me. Instead, like all who have appeared on television, I now wore at all times an expression of fatuous affability. This was in my case seasoned with a pinch of apprehension. Even today, when my name is called from a doorway, from a van or from the scaffolding round some building, I am never certain that, if I turn to acknowledge the greeting, I may not be spattered with a fusillade of abuse.

Philip Mackie, though white-haired, remains bouncy, amazingly young and eager to know everything you are willing to tell him. His scenario was written from a perusal of my autobiography and at least six hours of taped conversation with me during which he sat with the book open on his thigh, his finger on the page and his bright blue eyes on whatever passage interested him. When I was shown the script that had been composed from all this interrogation, I was disappointed. The result seemed curiously undigested, unresolved. One afternoon he had asked me what my father looked like. I had replied, 'Like Lewis Stone.' Accordingly the scenario contained the stage instruction 'Enter Quentin's father looking like Lewis Stone.' I had imagined that my jumbled speech would be translated into deathless prose. It was not until I saw the television play itself that I realized what common sense should have told me at once. Mr Mackie had simply wasted no time on anything that could not be used on the screen. I now saw that writing for a visual medium is in a kind of shorthand.

In spite of what world authorities have since judged to be the excellence of his work, Mr Mackie was compelled to run hatless through the streets of London for four long, dark years trying to raise sufficient funds to make a movie of his script.

In a voice so faint that I could not be thought to be about to make an offer, I once asked how much money was required. 'Three-quarters of a million dollars?' I hazarded, my lips trembling with the effort needed to utter such daring numerals. 'Wouldn't be nearly enough,' Mr Mackie replied coolly. 'They would have to be pounds.' Secretly I would have thought that Elizabeth Taylor could have been persuaded to act the part of me for a fee as large as that but I said nothing. Finance was never one of my strong subjects.

There was apparently a moment when an unnamed tycoon offered to produce the necessary cash if Danny La Rue could be induced to play the lead. I was delighted with this idea. 'Could it not', I asked, 'be made into a musical?' My proposal was laughed to scorn and the search for unconditional backing went blindly on. Seven years were to pass before my suggestion was taken seriously.

After a few months I forgot about the entire project and went back to the humble task of completing my book about style. It was finished, I think, in 1972 but this too turned out to be a bomb with a very long fuse. It did not see the light of day for another three years. Sad to say by that time its publisher and my actress friend had become estranged. We never all jumped up and down together.

During the past twelve crowded years, assistance has been given to me from so many and such diverse sources that it is not always possible for me to tell my tale chronologically. Occasionally I am forced to work in chain stitch, dragging forward into the present threads from the past.

When my agent fled to Texas, he left the matter of his correspondence in the hands of a Hungarian of 1956 vintage who lived in the flat above him and with whom he had become friendly. Some letters – ones, for instance, that said 'I love you, I love you' – the Texan wished to receive in America. Others, of lesser interest or none, he hoped could be answered or ignored without any decision from him. Into this latter category fell cheques for seven shillings and sixpence which represented my dwindling royalties on *The Naked Civil Servant*.

So it came about that I began to receive telephone calls and letters from my ex-agent's friend and, after a while, an invitation to visit him. These two men knew one another only because they were vertical neighbours and I met the second only because he agreed to deal with the letters of the first. This is but another instance of how tenuous has been the connection between the people and events that have furthered my progress.

At our first or second meeting, the Hungarian

64

said, 'I will be your agent.' For years we had no written agreement whatsoever. Those years would have been lean indeed if his wife had not fed me and had he not twisted and turned in a frenzied effort to find magazines and newspapers to which I could contribute quips, puns, anecdotes and perverse expressions of opinion.

In the summer of 1975 an afternoon came when, in a dreamy voice, my new agent told me that he had found himself with some money to spare and was thinking of putting on a play – presumably as the quickest way of getting rid of it. The theatre on which he finally settled for this venture was a room behind the King's Head in Islington. How to fill the evenings had already been decided but there were still the lunch-time opening hours to be occupied – if possible, profitably.

'I thought you could go on then,' he said. I was amazed.

'With what object, my good man?' I enquired.

'You could talk to people.'

'What about?'

'Doesn't really matter,' my agent replied. 'You needn't say the same thing each day.' Then he went to Spain.

Thus it was that, alone and totally unprepared, I tottered into the profession of public speaking.

At this point the already bewildering cast of this book is augmented by Mr Jackson. In the telephone book he is billed as being in personal management but I think he sits in a tower overlooking the centre of London like a ranger perched above the tree tops of a spruce forest in

Canada. Instead of watching for suspicious wisps of smoke, Mr Jackson waits to see if the lights go out in any West End theatre. The moment they do, he is there offering to fill whatever gap has occurred. It was he who presented me at the King's Head and, incidentally, he who provided me with a daily glass of whisky which has ever since been a feature of my stage appearances.

The drama upon which my agent had decided to lavish his superfluous wealth was called *Madame de Sade*. Though written by a Japanese gentleman called Mr Mishima about a Frenchwoman, it was constructed upon Greek lines. No action took place on stage; the audience was informed what had happened or was warned what was about to happen but always elsewhere.

The play failed. Not even the magnificent presence of Miss Chasen, striding up and down in thigh boots and brandishing a whip as long as Upper Street, was enough to satisfy modern English appetites. Nowadays people wish to see such a fascinating weapon used, preferably on the person sitting next to them.

Earlier in the day at the same venue, I too was fighting a losing battle. I frequently found myself haranguing a multitude of three people. When, after three weeks, the evening performances ceased, I asked if I might be spared further humiliation.

The subject upon which I had decided to lavish my rhetorical deficiencies was 'Life Style'. It served two purposes simultaneously. Firstly, it provided me with a vague framework within which I was able to talk to audiences about their own foibles which I was sure they would find more amusing than mine. Secondly, it was a suitable topic to illustrate, upon which, while writing the book, I had accumulated a number of anecdotes which I could use to dramatize my discourse.

Although my stay at the King's Head could loosely be called a disaster, I learned a great deal from it. For me it would never be easier to say different things on different days. I hardly vary my parrot cries in real life; on the stage I would never be able to find sufficient material. My experience of the world has been too limited, my understanding of that experience too shallow. Moreover I discovered that, while uttering one sentence, it was necessary to have a clear idea of what the next one would be so that I could concentrate not on what was to come but on the sounds already in my mouth. I found that I needed to pay great attention to their pitch, their volume and even to the length of the silences between them. This newly acquired knowledge did not later prevent the gay newspapers of New York from saying that I recited passages from my books not very well and in a whining voice but matters would, I am sure, have been even worse if my entire performance had been an improvisation.

I cannot claim that, if I had known early in life how my declining years were to be spent, I would at any time have enrolled my name for classes in voice production. I would never have had either the nerve or the money. When I was at my preparatory school my teachers subjected my

67

corrected cockney accent to limp ridicule and that was all the help I was given. How I wish now that they had tried to increase my vocal range or volume or both! As they did not I stagger on, flaunting my defects where I cannot conceal them.

Although using material from *How To Have a Life Style* on stage was a godsend, it also proved to be a trap. Working even loosely from something already written seduced me not only into quoting the same jokes from the same pages each day but also into arriving by the same number of paces at the same position on the platform to deliver them. I knew that such behaviour was unforgivable but seemed unable to resist it. The audience was probably unaware of what I was doing but there was a young man employed to sit by the door and prevent latecomers from creeping in without paying. It was when I passed him that I bowed my head in shame. I found out later that this was unnecessary. He was an actor and inured to the embarrassment of witnessing feigned spontaneity. To offset this old-fashioned element of slickness, I tried to roughen the edges of the show with various cute tricks. I marched straight out of the street on to the platform and paced up and down it until given a sign that it was time to begin but, in spite of all these ruses, a certain staginess gradually seeped into the situation.

In real life I was moving stealthily towards respectability but, in theatrical terms, I was losing my innocence with alarming rapidity considering that I was surprised to find myself on the stage at all. This reaction, however, was not shared by others. When I announced to my friends that I had gone into the public speaking racket, they only sighed. 'When', they asked, 'did you ever do anything else?'

Six

The television rights in *The Naked Civil Servant* were sold for £350. When audiences appear to imagine that my financial status has recently been altered out of all recognition, I mention this sum; I like to hear them gasp. All the same this is not a hard-luck story. During my entire working life, never, over a long period, did I earn more than £12 a week. That £350 meant a great deal to me and I am grateful for a deal which was so conscientiously, so scrupulously, transacted, although it took over four years to complete.

I do not remember exactly how I received the news that Thames Television had bought Mr Mackie's script but I do recall that, when it was arranged that I should meet the director of the play, I was taken all the way to Teddington by taxi. At that time I had had so little experience of television that I was amazed by the extravagance of this method of transport. At Teddington Studios, besides Mr Gold, the director, I was introduced to Mr Hurt who was soon to become my representative on earth. He said, 'I have no intention of merely giving a vaudeville imitation of Mr

Crisp.' I was somewhat relieved by this remark.

This occasion, social, pleasant, informal, was in fact the turning point of the tide against which I had been swimming for more than sixty years. I was on my way back to becoming a virgin. More than that, after a lifetime of condemnation for my sexual deviation, that very fact was to be used to present me to the world as being of interest for human reasons that transcended my sin.

Very kindly, so that I might earn money under the heading of technical advice, I was allowed on to four of the locations where the film was being photographed. First I saw the scene where the child dances in front of the mirror. This seemed difficult to get just right because to my surprise the boy looked not at his reflection but at the director. Later in the day I was taken to Richmond where John Hurt's club membership card was torn up. On other occasions I also witnessed the meeting in the café and the art class. Only in this last place did I offer advice. I feared that Mr Hurt might not know what an operatic business posing can become if you fling yourself into it. I needn't have bothered; he himself was an art student in a time gone by.

I could not get used to the intensity with which the entire team cared whether the production was like my life or not. I had supposed that all that was needed was for some such person as I once was to be seen surviving some such events as I once experienced. I should have known that, if you show the members of an art department a real person, they go mad. They have spent so many long hours peering at faded group photographs in which the third schoolboy from the left is rumoured to be some famous politician. Now, at last, their subject was appallingly distinct. They could work at something that would yield demonstrable proof of their skills. They took pictures of me from above, from below, from the left and from the right. They even took me to a shop in Burlington Street so that the wig-maker there would be able to reconstruct the architecture of my hair. At one time or another during his performance, Mr Hurt wore five wigs in order to pass from innocence (a rich mouse colour) through depravity (scarlet) to senility (discreet mauve).

People often ask me if I worked with Mr Hurt before he began to play the part of me. It is difficult to imagine what any such sessions would have been like but we do not have to try. I met him only twice before he began to make the teleplay – once, as described, at Teddington and a second time when he and his true love invited me to dinner at their home in Flask Walk. I mentioned the difficulty an actor might have in playing a victim of fate because, in an extremely competitive profession, he must in real life cultivate every ounce of aggression of which his nature is capable in order to stay in work. He disagreed and he should know. In *10 Rillington Place* he portrayed Christopher Evans, the all-time victim. Never during the evening did I say (nor would I have dared to say) that my host might try doing this or that while acting *The Naked Civil Servant*, yet when I finally saw the teleplay, I noticed that he had included in his characterization all sorts of tiny details. He had mastered the Red Indian's walk and, as he drifted along the streets of London, he held his fingers straight rather than slightly curved as ordinary mortals do.

When Mr Mackie told me that he had found someone to play the part of me he added, 'I've never seen anyone so willing to play a part.' I suggested that if you were to show anyone in the entertainment business a book in which almost every paragraph begins with the word 'I' he will be anxious to play the lead in it, but I now think that in Mr Mackie's portrait of me John Hurt saw some special opportunity. If he was led to do this by instincts, they did not betray him. He won an award.

When you meet him in real life, Mr Hurt seems shorter than I and he is actually much slighter. He looks pale, frail and very tired. The naturally drooping eyelids, together with having his eyebrows plucked from underneath by the make-up department, gave him on the screen the scornful look that in earlier life I was so often accused of wearing.

John Osborne, whom I once met at a party, suddenly turned on me with the words, 'You've made sure that young man never gets another good part.' In fact the reverse was true. Since making *The Naked Civil Servant* Hurt has hardly ever been out of work. For this reason, and because my own life has recently become more occupied than I ever thought it would be, it is unlikely that I shall ever know him well but I shall always be grateful to him for the immense tact with which he presented me to the world. It is easy to imitate other people and especially easy to imitate me. The whole production might at any moment have become a scream but because of him this was avoided. In any situation, however bizarre, he never saw himself as the camp scarecrow that I seem to other people to be. Instead, he worked from within to reveal me as the helpless victim of a misguided dream.

I saw *The Naked Civil Servant* when it was shown to the press before it was televised. At least I saw almost all of it. The car sent to take me to the Thames Studios in Euston Road was late. I could easily have travelled by bus and been punctual but already I was becoming accustomed to the crazy luxury of the media. I was very worried upon that occasion because I knew that, immediately the film was over, I would be questioned by the critics – and journalists don't want answers, they want jokes. The best that I could manage was to say that the television presentation of my life was better than the real thing because it was so much shorter.

When the play was flashed before the unsuspecting eyes of the public, I saw it with some friends. In a calmer mood by then, I tried to judge it purely as entertainment. This was not easy because it was the kind of programme that, had I been in no way personally involved, I would never have watched in a million years. I have long since ceased to be interested in homosexuality as a subject; there just doesn't seem anything left to say about it. In spite of this I was well aware of what an excellent play had been produced. The unresolved quality that I thought I had perceived in Mr Mackie's script had completely evaporated. The narrative moved slowly but relentlessly forward. Even the captions, which when they were first proposed I could not take seriously, seemed wholly integrated into the mode of telling the story.

I have been asked if there was any detail in which the play differed from my actual past. The question has recurred so often that, after a while, because my whole nature revolts against saying nothing, I searched for some point of deviation however trivial. At length I dredged up the fact at one moment in the play Mr Hurt tells one of his persecutors to sod off. Not only would I never have used such a word (which would have sounded far more unladylike then than now) but no one as habitually acquiescent as I would have risked this gesture of defiance in a situation so obviously dangerous. I made this observation in Mr Hurt's presence. He delighted me by protesting that he had said the words very nicely.

The day after *The Naked Civil Servant* was shown to the public I was interviewed by Mavis Nicholson, the darling of afternoon television. I had been looked over beforehand so the event did not come as a great surprise, nor did Mrs Nicholson. I had often watched her questioning minor celebrities and thought her just like home but prettier. The interview that I remembered best was the one during which she sat between two very discreet homosexual men and asked them if it was true that men find it difficult to form lasting emotional relationships. They gave the conventional reply that in society there are so many bonds

76

that keep heterosexual couples together and so many forces that drive gay men apart. I regretted that neither interviewee had said that he was glad that, owing to his temperament and his position in society, he was free forever from the damp, dark prison of eternal love. I must have written these words somewhere because, when we met, Mrs Nicholson quoted them.

I regarded my meeting with Mrs Nicholson before the public interview as an opportunity to set her mind at rest. It is always the interviewer who has more to lose than the interviewee. The latter can say what he likes so long as he does not expect ever to appear on television again. The interrogator, on the other hand, is the employee of a vast corporation with a carefully guarded public image and, if by some awful chance something treasonable or blasphemous is said, he may be held responsible.

Mrs Nicholson said that she did not know what questions to ask me. I assured her that I would not be shocked or embarrassed by anything that she might say and that in my replies I would never use the shortest words for the longest things.

Our interview turned out to be one of the best I have ever had and the highest point of it came when by mistake I allowed the word 'camp' to fall from my lips. 'Do you think your little friends will understand the word?' I asked, nodding towards the world beyond the camera. Mrs Nicholson leaned forward to give the lens a searching look. 'I should think so,' she said in a slightly cynical voice.

In my first interview on *Late Night Line-Up*, I

had only wanted my replies to be heard, understood and, by a miracle, believed. By the time this second programme was promised I wanted more than that. I wished to add what I am to what I said. To some extent I desired to have the situation on my own terms. Mrs Nicholson never tried to prevent this from happening; indeed she aided and abetted me.

I had taken to watching other people being interviewed – not in order to hear what they had to say but in the hope of discovering techniques for dealing with the special hazards of this highly artificial form of self-presentation. What is needed is some way of talking intimately with the interviewer while acknowledging that we are both on display. If, for instance, I am asked whether or not I like writing books, I cannot pass my hand across my brow and say that my genius is a great burden to me. I am in the presence of millions of people some of whom may get up at four every morning to milk cows while I rise at ten and sit by the fire making a few unusable notes.

Although I never questioned him about it, I imagine that when, worn out with trudging the unrelenting pavements of Wardour Street, Mr Mackie at length accepted Thames Television's offer, he may have felt that he was settling for less than his original dream of seeing his scenario made into a real film.

Certainly I, though glad of any outcome to his heroic persistence, was slightly deflated because I am so mad about the movies.

Since then I have changed my mind.

Financially there can be no comparison. If *The Naked Civil Servant* had become a picture, I need never have stepped out of bed again but, in other respects, television has advantages that movies lack. If a film has a homosexual theme, it is heavily advertised as such. In consequence it is seen only by gay people and liberals wishing to be observed going into and coming out of the cinema where it is being shown. On television I reached a more mixed audience.

Books and plays are diversions about which most of us exercise some decision even if our selection is based on totally misleading publicity. The movies are in a twilit zone. A woman may save up time and money to spend on a film of which she has very definite expectations or she may flop into the nearest cinema to fill in time between the end of a shopping orgy and the beginning of a train journey back to Chorley Wood. Television is even lower down the scale of human choice. We nearly always see it by default.

In my mind's ear I hear a housewife calling from the kitchen to her husband in the living-room.

'What's on now, luv?'

'The queers.'

'What's on the other side?'

'The news.'

'Oh Gawd. As you were.'

In some such circumstances as these, my life story was unfurled before the eyes of people who until that moment had never given a serious thought to the subject of homosexuality.

I have pondered deeply the difference between

the public reaction to Granada's documentary and to the play shown by Thames Television. The telephone calls provoked by the former were contemptuous or hostile; by the latter, mixed. The letters that I received after the first were negligible; those that followed the second were kind, sometimes laudatory. The manner of strangers encountered in the street subsequent to the first programme was uneasy; after the second it was a subtle blend of curiosity and forgiveness.

Some people have attributed these differences to the passage of time between 1969 and 1975 but there has been very little profound change in morals since the war. While my book was in the process of being published, amendments were being made to the law concerning homosexuality and someone said to me, 'They'll make a lot of difference to you.' This remark was kindly intended but absurd. No one has ever pointed the finger of scorn at me and cried, 'Look at him, he's illegal.' If anything the piratical element in my predicament was an advantage. It appealed to all outsiders who, for quite different reasons, despised the conventions. The English hated me for being effeminate and, in a country where women are still to some extent despised, this attitude has not altered.

The gradual and very slight change that we have witnessed during the past thirty years has occurred because more and more power has passed into the hands of the young or, to be more accurate, a louder and louder voice has begun to issue from their lips. Teenagers have always been interested in gaining more sexual freedom than their parents wished them to have and have never been keen on acquiring the social leverage that their elders constantly recommend. Now they can say so. In other words, we have not moved into a permissive society: the young are just as stuffy in their own way as adults. We are merely stuck with an outspoken society.

Since neither I in the documentary nor Mr Hurt in the teleplay flashed you-know-what before the cameras and since neither of us uttered obscenities we might both by modern standards be considered old-fashioned – even pre-war. In this respect the two programmes were therefore equal and, since in the first my sins were only discussed and in the second they were acted out, the latter, at least in the eyes of older viewers, must have seemed the more immoral of the two yet the reaction to it was more benign.

I think the answer lies largely with the press. Critics will, I am sure, agree that they have no power to change minds that are already made up but they can reorientate the ditherers. When one journalist went so far as to say that the Thames programme justified the existence of television, she made it legitimate for even the most refined taste to have enjoyed itself and when Clive James (of all people) said that the protagonist in *The Naked Civil Servant* appeared to be 'some kind of a hero', amusement was nudged in the direction of condonation.

I cannot deny that I was surprised at the unqualified praise lavished upon the teleplay. I had feared that one or two critics at least would point out the degree of depravity in my life story. In fact no mention was made of this. I was pleased that no opprobrium had fallen on the makers of the programme and my pleasure turned to delight when I found that some of the glory properly meant for the play itself was descending like golden rain upon me. The redemptive element in television was beginning to work in my favour.

It is also true that the sheer bulk of critical opinion and therefore of general discussion caused my existence to impinge upon even the most sluggish consciousness. As my agent said, 'You must accept the fact that you will become part of the fantasies of total strangers.'

The teleplay in which I had appeared for about a minute and a half came to be called my programme. This was not because my presence was in any way dramatically effective but because, from being constantly photographed, my image became recognizable – as unchanging as a stuffed bird, though not as silent – an object of ridicule to schoolboys and of curiosity to taxi drivers.

At first this latter reaction was a source of wonderment to me but, after a little reflection, I saw that it was natural – even inevitable. If you have driving skills and you don't like people, you find a job as a long-distance lorry driver. On those seemingly interminable nocturnal hauls you need speak to no one and meet no one except hitch-hikers whom you ravish and whose used bodies you fling like empty Yorkie wrappers into the hedges. If, however, you do like people, you acquire a taxi. Whom then will you meet? The rich, the famous and the desperate.

Bit by bit, a taxi at a time, I was becoming the almost acceptable face of homosexuality.

When the laws of England were being changed, market research into homosexuality was carried out. Nothing significant emerged from these enquiries but this. When asked what they would expect a gay man to look like, housewives replied, 'Oh, you know – actorish, effeminate, inclined to wear bright colours.' (Now they would merely say 'someone like Quentin'.) If, on the other hand, they had already admitted to knowing a homosexual man and were asked what he was like, they usually answered, 'Just like everyone else.'

Superficially the present fashion among gay men for normalizing their clothes and their mannerisms is a relief to the rest of the world. Socially it makes dealing with them less embarrassing but, deep down, this subdued public image makes heterosexuals uneasy. If gay men look like everyone else, then they may be anywhere – everywhere. How much safer to be able to see one coming from a mile away! It gives you time to make up your mind what to do – call the police, lock up the kids, scream with laughter or duck. This, of course, is what I told the whole world as far back as 1931 but then it paid no heed because, at that time, it did not realize that there were any queers other than the ones that could be spotted. Now that intimations of a large hidden minority have come to light, meeting an obvious pansy is almost a relief.

I do not merely infer that public attitudes towards me have softened. I have proof.

Recently I was standing at a bus stop in Shepherd's Bush when a lorry drew up on the opposite side of the street. The driver climbed slowly down from his cabin on to the ground, crossed the road and said, 'You're Quentin Crisp.' When I falteringly admitted that I was, he added, 'I get the hang of it now.' He meant that he had come to see homosexuality on my terms – as a desire to live as though one were a member of the opposite sex.

It is, of course, precisely this easily digested image, camp, ineffectual, slightly silly and, worst of all, almost indifferent to sex, that the gay community finds so distasteful. Aversion to it is so strong that *Gay News* expressed the opinion that it would have been better for 'The Cause' if *The Naked Civil Servant* had been published posthumously – a literary way of saying, 'Drop dead'.

It was not, however, the book that caused the rift between me and the great body of homosexuality.

While my identity remained in the form of written words, the Gay Movement (as distinct from gay people) accepted and to some extent welcomed it. The fact that a book in part about my sex life had been published at all was considered to be a tiny triumph for the cause even if my image did lack the aggression requisite for an era when protest was developing into a fad and the voice of minorities was becoming everywhere so shrill. As very slowly I moved from the written to the spoken word – as I ceased to be an idea and became an icon – certain attributes of my nature, which before could only have been inferred, became obvious. My struggle to ingratiate myself with the majorites grew to be horribly apparent.

I once went to address all the homosexuals in Westminster – not in the Houses of Parliament but in a public house called the Westminster Arms. During the meeting someone said to me, 'You used to be the Martin Luther King of the Movement. What are these Uncle Tom sentiments you now express?'

Never, even with a jolly laugh, would I have dared to compare myself with Mr King. Any endeavour to do so would not merely be presumptuous, it would be pointless. I was never militant. As I explained to the gentleman who asked me the question, if, in that far-off time, I sat on a bus next to a stranger and he ostentatiously moved away from me, I said, 'If you like, I will get out at the next stop but even people like me cannot walk everywhere.'

Public interest was beginning to be focussed on me just when the new image of gayness (by no means the same thing as gaiety) was being advertised. Homosexuals had not only modified their appearance, they were forever popping up on television to explain that they were really quite ordinary. In my opinion this ploy will never work. Except in the state of Illinois, ordinary people do not go about claiming – nay, boasting – that they are hum-drum. The declaration is chiefly interesting because it is the reverse of a previous posture.

In a time gone by, homosexuals, when challenged, used to rattle off a list of names of writers whom history claimed were gay. They seemed to derive self-assurance from a supposed kinship even though they, themselves, never wrote a word – not even home.

When I was young most men who indulged in any sort of sexual deviation went about their business – especially their monkey business – discreetly. The people who proclaimed their difference from the rest of the world did so, like me, because they had no real choice. Any other course of action would have demanded a life-time of perpetual self-watchfulness, as opposed to self-regard. Our brazenness was the solution to a personality problem rather than an explicitly sexual one.

This is difficult for young people nowadays to understand because sexual freedom has become more important than identity. Indeed it has superseded it. The modern philosophy states, 'I ejaculate therefore I am.' Those who now protest and demonstrate and march most persistently are often those with the least clearly marked personalities. Like cells in an organism, it takes thousands of teenagers to make up a single identity. They feel that it will be through numbers rather than willpower that they will at last become a force of which society must take some notice. The trouble with this method of trying to gain more liberty is that those who adopt it, instead of bowing to the laws of the community in general, must conform to the narrower and even less rewarding constraints of their chosen regiment.

There is a restaurant in New York in which there is not a woman to be seen. At any one time the place contains about forty men all of whom are between the ages of eighteen and twenty-eight, or wish they were. All are wearing tractor boots, pre-ruined jeans, kitchen tablecloth shirts, and little scrubby moustaches. The only way in which an intruder can tell that he has not accidentally stumbled into the canteen of a building site is because everybody looks so clean. These young men *look* marvellous but, if we are speaking of personal liberty, they have taken a step forward only in that they have entered a more fashionable ghetto.

In England the craze for uniformity has passed into the realm of parody; manliness has given place to cruelty. (They were never so very far apart.) In Earl's Court there is an establishment where the entire clientele is dressed like the Wild One in black leather decorated with chains. Almost everyone present has remembered to carry a crash helmet but no one mentions that he has arrived at his destination by bus. Even as a sexual visiting card this gear is often totally misleading. In an encounter of the fourth kind, half these boys would turn out to be in search of nothing more bizarre than a little friendly sensuality.

I do not think that any of these antics is sinful. I complain only that they all confuse an issue that is already surrounded by misconceptions. I have never expressed the opinion that what modern homosexuals want they do not deserve. Whatever tricks they get up to I wish them well. I am also aware that what they demand they demand for others as well as for themselves. Thus an element of altruism is added to the call for justice. I have only tried to make two points. One is that, if anyone submerges his individuality in a group for the sake of gaining political acknowledgement of his mere sexual needs, he may find that he has thrown away the larger part of his personal freedom. I also fear that the ultimate outcome of too much militancy shown by any minority may not be what is hoped. This stridency creates panic in the majority and brings about a fierce confrontation between the gay people and the sad people. This can only re-open that hideous chasm between them that time and boredom were just beginning so conveniently to fill in.

When I was working in Newhaven, a psychiatrist invited me to spend a day at his home. I had a wonderful time but, at the outset, was worried by the fact that, as he drove through the town, all his spare attention was given to pointing out which bars were gay or had been gay, which restaurants were straight though run by homosexuals and so on. I know that psychiatrists must deal in what is not in what might be, but I was disturbed by the kind of glee with which he surveyed the ugly rift between two warring factions. I longed to ask my host if he was not yearning for the day when he would be able to frequent a bar simply because it was near or warm or quiet. It seems to me that the Kinsey Report counts for nothing if we have not learned that the answer to the question 'Are you queer?' is no longer the desperate cry 'I am, I am', but merely a polite 'Not today, thank you.' My host's imagination seemed to dwell with alarming intensity upon the rituals of that sex-sodden monastery which, even when I was young, I hated. I would not then and I will not now accept the notion that, if someone has not been propositioned by eleven o'clock on Friday night, his week has been wasted.

I urgently feel that, if gay people want to be happy, they must vacate their secret world, they must stop frightening not only the horses but also their riders. They must recognize that it is in the very nature of integration that you cannot fight for it. You can only wait. Mr Lustgarten, who practically invented crime, has pointed out that it is not the law that changes public opinion, it is public opinion which very gradually modifies the law. If homosexuals prematurely bring about the passing of a law for which society is not ready, they will earn its hatred. Anyone who demands acceptance places himself in the same position as a girl who asks, 'Do you really love me?' Every mature woman knows where that gets her. It is more than forty years now since I presumed to think that I represented homosexuality. Since then I have come to realize that I represent nothing grander than my puny self. This does not mean that I have in any way connived at the hostility of the gay world. Especially in New York I was sorry to find that I had made enemies. If this saddens me less now than formerly, it may be because I have recently acquired more friends among heterosexuals. On the stage in America I was often asked how the gay scene in New York compares with that of London. It was a question I couldn't answer because I'm never there. My journey has not taken me deeper and deeper into the jungle but mercifully out into the common light of day.

I will not be nudged into a quarrel with the human race. Now that we've finally met, I love it.

Seven

The difference between my life before and after *The Naked Civil Servant* was broadcast became most clearly visible at the King's Head. When I returned there in the spring of 1976, the little huddle of embarrassed friends sitting at one table had become a crowd so numerous that some members of the audience were obliged to lean against the back wall of the room for an hour holding empty beer glasses and the plates on which their pork pies had stood.

Lunch-time theatre-goers in public houses are not only drinkers whose feet are killing them and who want to sit down anywhere at almost any price, people gather from far and wide and even from high and low. On one occasion, Mrs Churchill brought Lady Diana Cooper who looked magnificent in a huge black hat, as though she were in mourning for Ascot.

As far as I know the phenomenon of lunch-time theatre has never been explained. During the war it was justified by the fact that many people were reluctant to go out in the evening. They either found the black-out too confusing or the aerial bombardment too frightening. Now that these adverse conditions no longer prevail, why has such an obviously inconvenient form of entertainment returned?

Undoubtedly it is part of the general de-glamorization of show business. It accords with the modern notion that anyone can entertain. Get yourself a guitar and you'll be a pop star in no time. But in fact, theatre in a very confined space is acknowledged by professionals to present its own particular difficulties. There can be no anxious glances into the wings to see what on earth has delayed your leading man; there must be no nervous trembling of the hands except for drama-tic purposes; no perspiration must appear on the brow. The entire audience is so close that details like these can easily be seen. Actors only do this work because they must. Employment is so hard to find that they will adapt themselves to whatever conditions are imposed upon them. In lunch-time theatre they will force themselves to act with the same attention to detail that they would display before the television cameras.

Lunch-time entertainment is welcomed by impresarios as well as by starving actors. It provides as many showcases as Burlington Arcade and at half the price. It is a place where a protégée can be seen performing in a properly-lighted area before an audience that has paid to see her. For all concerned this is at least a fairer test of histrionic ability than sitting in a producer's office crying, 'Woe unto Ilium'.

All these advantages to individuals who are in or

on the periphery of show business do not, however, explain why real people attend these events. It must be very inconvenient for a girl to fling the cover over her typewriter and dash through the streets snatching up a sandwich en route like a Polish lancer displaying his horsemanship. Nevertheless I know that women in full employment came to hear me. On one occasion a girl started to leave before the end. When I implored her not to go – even offering to say the opposite if she would stay – she replied in a mournful voice, 'I have to go back to work.' It seems strange that, for such a fragment of diversion, anyone would risk incurring her boss's displeasure with her unpunctuality and start an afternoon's drudgery wracked by indigestion and with a heart pounding from having run all the way along Upper Street, yet some people have not found the price too great.

Perhaps there is no mystery. Possibly lunch-time theatre is merely blindly following a fashion set by the Edinburgh Festival. There entertainment starts at half-past eleven in the morning and covers every available horizontal surface (of which there are not many in Scotland's capital). This welter of frivolity in the grimmest city on earth was something of which at that time I had barely heard. Soon I was to experience it.

I have been to the Edinburgh Festival three times. The last time, I took part in the inaugural parade and sat in a coach beside a famous Scottish actress called Miss McArthur. Crowds lined the streets, leaned out of every available window and even climbed the trees along our route. As Miss McArthur smiled, bowed to right and left and waved, she said to me, 'We'll never work for a bigger audience than this.' She was right. I enjoyed myself enormously but, looking back, I think the year I liked the Festival most was my first in 1976 when everything about it was new to me.

That summer the city was ruled by Miss Greer. She was there to explain to the world the various events. She is very tall and quite formidable, an effect that she offsets by weaving into her public image an element of self-doubt. While she interviewed me sitting on a bench in some public gardens, she brushed the front of her dress and said to the technicians, 'I've got marmalade on my skirt.' This small gesture I took to be a manifestation of what Mr Tennyson called, 'craven fears of being great.'

I was working for a group of students from Bristol University. I occupied a room in one of the two huge flats which they had rented. Early one morning, Miss Greer visited us. The television crew that accompanied her everywhere woke up the students and told them to look as though they were asleep. When the sea of horizontal bodies had been photographed, we all sat round the kitchen table for a cornflakes session. I think the young people were required to be helpless waifs far from home. This is one of my favourite roles but the students seemed reluctant to co-operate. Perhaps they feared that their parents would watch the programme and that thereafter the hall would be knee deep in a snow of anxious letters. During this visit, Miss Greer was taken on a tour of inspection of the various rooms. When she beheld the dilapidated state of my hair brush, her heart was touched and she bought me a new one. Years later, she said to me, 'The way the press went on you would have thought it was of solid gold.' To me, of course, it *was* solid gold.

Every fringe theatre in Edinburgh is full because, out of loyalty to the profession, all the actors who are not on their own stages are in the auditoria of their colleagues. The Heriot-Watt theatre where I worked was no exception. On my very first day, when I asked the audience if it had understood and, furthermore, believed me, a man sitting right at the back of the house complained that I had not, as he had hoped, conducted a serious existential discussion. I apologized and explained that he must not imagine that, because I was smiling, I did not at any time say what I did not mean. Seated beside this gentleman was his wife or worse. She asked if she could not have a life style which included her children. I pointed out that the trouble with children was that they were not returnable. When the audience seemed to find this remark amusing, the unknown orator deflected his rage from me to the people around him. 'You're sycophants!' he cried but his enemies were not to be cowed. For the first time I then realized the truth of a statement made in her autobiography by Miss Bergman, that people come to the theatre hoping, longing to be entertained; they want performers to succeed. They certainly do not come primarily to be informed.

Now that I have had more experience of public speaking, I know that I should have invited the heckler down on to the stage. We could have had a debate which would have enlivened the afternoon miraculously. At the time I only waited feebly for the storm to pass.

During that first week in Edinburgh, I was summoned back to London by Thames Television so that I might appear on a programme with Mr Hurt and Mrs Whitehouse. The umpire was Mr Cavett. After the show, when we were in the drinking room, he said that, if I ever went to the States, he would invite me on to his own programme. Such a possibility seemed very remote then.

I admire Mrs Whitehouse though I do not suppose that my adulation is something that the lady seeks. She knows exactly what she is doing. Just as Miss Greer uses self-doubt to soften her personality so Mrs Whitehouse adds to her puritanical image a pinch of sensuality. On the evening when I met her she was wearing a brick red suit, she had curly hair and her slightly pouting lips were painted a pale orange. These adornments that ran counter to the public's idea of her would lose her a few marks were she being judged as a stylist but, as the adjuncts of an evangelist, they work in her favour. If she wore dull clothes, had thin lips and scraped her hair back from her brow, the world would say, 'Look at her. No wonder she's against sex.' She has seen to it that this sort of comment shall not be made. She is watchful not only of what she looks like but also of what she says. When asked if she found *The Naked Civil Servant* shocking, she replied that she did not and added that she thought the programme had been sympathetically made and that she had learned a great deal from it. Mrs Whitehouse never puts a foot wrong.

Going to Edinburgh was not my first visit to Scotland. I had already been for a day a night and a day to St Andrews to talk to the university students.

There is no railway station at St Andrews. When they built the famous golf course, they removed all hope of reaching it. Instead I arrived at a place called Leuchars. Standing on the station platform I found myself in a typically Hitchcockian setting. All around me the land was as flat as Texas and no matter where I looked I saw no sign of human life. If the sinister crop-sprayer flies overhead, I thought, I shall have no sugar canes among which to hide. Fortunately some students came to meet me with a car. Immediately I found them more relaxed than their equivalents in England. The reason for this had already been explained to me by Mr Coren who then ruled the university but who now rules *Punch*. 'The young of St Andrews never march,' he told me. 'There are only two streets to march along and they never carry banners because the wind is too strong.'

St Andrews is built on the very edge of the world – not by the sea but overhanging it. The whole town bristles with cannon emplacements, is riddled with dungeons and encrusted with ruins. The traditional English view of the Scots must have been based on the landscape. In fact the inhabitants not only of St Andrews but of everywhere that I have been in Scotland are communicative, laughter-loving and indulgent with foreigners to the verge of folly.

On my way back to real life, I was shown the beauties of Edinburgh by a friend of mine who rules Waverley Station. He is devoted to antiquity. Pointing with a Charlie's Aunt umbrella to a row of houses the colour of atomic ash, he said, 'Modern 1820s stuff.' To me the greatest delight of that hilarious sight-seeing tour was the river. The Leith has mossy banks, is canopied by tall trees, bejewelled with emerald green subaqueous ferns and runs laughing through the forbidden city.

Arriving back in London I reckoned that I had travelled for over eighteen hours in order to speak for two but it had all been worth it.

Eight

Once, during a childhood holiday, an aeroplane landed in a field behind whatever seaside resort my parents had chosen for that year. As soon as the inevitable crowd had collected, a tout started to sell five-shilling tickets for a short air trip. My sister and I queued up, were whisked round a few neighbouring fields for about five minutes and were then returned to earth. As so often happens if I recall any childhood experience, I remember trying to feel the appropriate emotion. I wanted to be afraid or, at least, amazed, as the wind rushed past my ears and the world dipped beneath me. I did not succeed.

More than fifty years were to pass before I again travelled by air. This time it was to make my mad dash from Scotland to London and back for my brief meeting with Mr Cavett. This journey was a little more exciting. Flying machines, I discovered, had become heavier and, when they leave the ground, it is possible by an effort of identification, to share with them their struggle to gain altitude. I found air travel to be a mode of transport that I enjoyed, so, when invited to go to Belfast, I had no qualms. Once you've done one festival, I thought, you've done them all. I was wrong. Going by plane to Ireland is a slightly different experience. The amount of time spent in the sky is about the same as when you visit Scotland but the number of hours occupied by wandering round the airport is greater. I think that there is only one plane making the Belfast run. If it hasn't returned, you wait. If you haven't any crossword puzzles to do, you can always spend the time being searched so thoroughly that you are even required to take off your hat and you may have everything you are carrying taken from you – even your umbrella. 'What', I asked, 'could I do with that which would be considered immoral or subversive?' I received no reply.

The Festival of Northern Ireland relies heavily on that one vehicle shuttling to and from England. If it doesn't arrive on time, programmes have to be altered or even cancelled. I was two hours late but that hardly mattered as I was not due to perform until the early evening. I was met by an organizer and taken into the city by a circuitous route. The driver explained that it was prettier than the more direct route. I dutifully admired the scenery but I knew that what she meant was that on this route we were less likely to be questioned.

My arrival, like that of any British person, was regarded as a gesture of affirmation – almost as a message of hope. The organizers of the festival were very concerned that I should be treated well. Even so, once in Belfast, there was hardly time to eat. Every moment until my first performance was taken up with interviews. The press was not hostile but the questions it put to me were less bland than they had been in Edinburgh. I was asked if it worried me that people might come to see me out of mere curiosity. In fact that is the reason why I am watched by audiences anywhere — to see how anyone so wicked can still move and speak — but I replied that the spirit in which the public arrived was less crucial than its mood when it left.

The weather was more predictable than the interviews. It rained. The sky was incessantly wracked by dark, swiftly moving clouds like the tattered flags of a defeated rabble.

All this I had expected. My first real shock was finding that the façades of both the television stations were ironclad like the sides of battleships. Once, presumably, they were resplendent with wide glass doors, a few marble steps and a long enquiry desk. Now there was an opening no wider than the front door of an ordinary house. When this was unlocked I saw almost immediately behind it another door. In between the two there was just room for me, my escort and the janitor. If we had shot him, the second door would not have been opened. Except that the small space was not filled with water, it was like the Davis device of a submarine. I realized then how great was the city's terror of inflammatory propaganda. If any un-authorized person could have reached the microphones to say that the pope was infallible and that the city had fallen, panic would have set in. In London we would know that it was Mr Welles having us on but there the effect would be disastrous.

My audience on my first evening consisted almost entirely of women. They were very attentive but were made uneasy by almost everything I said – even though I remembered not to mention You-Know-Who or the pope. When someone complained that she couldn't possibly do any of the things I recommended because she had to hurry home to cook a meal for her husband and three sons, I said, 'Leave them.' The whole room gasped. An English audience would only have smiled. It is difficult for us to comprehend that the people of Northern Ireland are ruled by a regime that is less concerned with morality than with religious doctrine. Their sectarianism is so divisive that, if you say you are an atheist, they ask, 'But is it the God of the Catholics or the God of the Protestants in whom you do not believe?' Apart from their religious beliefs, the poor, in Ireland, as everywhere else, seem chiefly concerned with living to the next day. It is the rich who are worried about the fair name of their country. At a posh party I attended, before I had uttered a word someone had protested, 'Things are not as bad as they are made out to be.' The terrible truth is that there is a sense in which the troubles are not bad enough. Life can go on indefinitely absorbing a few more pointless deaths every day. No major decision is forced upon anyone and, if it were, what would it be? When you ask the young people there what they want, they reply, 'To be left alone.' They have no desire to be annexed by Holy Ireland nor do they wish to be part of England. They want to be the inhabitants of Northern Ireland. Perhaps the solution to the whole problem would be to give the place an entirely new, non-inflammable name.

On the evening when I was not working, I was taken to a banquet given by the city's gay population. They are angry and no wonder. They have to bear the shame of being part of the British Empire while reaping none of the benefits of its genial depravity but even there, as in so many places on earth, the quarrel is less with the law than with the police. You might think that the constabulary of Ulster had enough to do just staying alive but no. It finds time to chivvy the gay men incessantly. One young man had been held in a police station for hours 'on suspicion'. No complainant had come forward to state that he had been corrupted; no time or place had been specified when or where the crime was supposed to have occurred. I would say that, by any standards, this procedure would be classed as harassment.

I had gone to Northern Ireland not exactly to be shot but certainly in the hope of being shot at. I was beginning to realize that, though some may have publicity thrust upon them, I was someone who must achieve it. I jumped up and down in front of the soldiers but they ran away.

Because of the various festivals, I was starting, in a very small way, to travel. I had never envied people who went abroad. I knew that the experiences that they described as so pleasurable would for me be uncomfortable or might lead to humiliation. My relationship with the English was dodgy enough. With the inhabitants of a foreign country it might be downright frightening. Those of my friends who took their holidays outside Britain, usually went to France. They either spoke tourist French without any apparent feeling of degradation or they were content to wave their arms and offer less which, in Paris, is practically a full-time occupation. The ostensible object of these vacations was either sight-seeing or, if they were spent on the Mediterranean coast, sun-bathing. The first of these pastimes tires me; the second makes me positively ill. The real purpose of these holidays abroad was to air a sophisticated preference for a continental way of life which, to the English before the Common Market opened, represented culture or art – two more causes of fatigue and nausea. Abroad, in those days I felt, had nothing to offer me.

Now at the festivals I saw that foreign countries need not be irritating regions where I would be compelled to sit around wondering what people were saying about me. If carefully selected they could be new worlds to conquer or, at least, new worlds to con. I also discovered that the appalling anxieties attendant upon getting from one country to the next could be delegated to others.

Within two years of my first timid departures from England, I was in a situation where these conditions were nearly always fulfilled.

Among the men who interviewed me in Northern Ireland was a Mr Rafferty. When I returned to England after my first visit to New York, we met again. This time, on the Mohammed principle, he came to Britain for the purpose of preparing a radio programme on the invasion of privacy. He wished to start this project with me because he judged that my opinions on the subject would be the most extreme.

He was right. What is privacy for if not for invading?

By now, I am happy to say, I have no private life. I want none. Like most people who are not quintuplets, I started out with one but, a little at a time, I have divested myself of it as a traveller abandons superfluous luggage when he sees that the night is coming and his destination is still a long way off. I quite understand Miss Loren's indignation at being photographed in church at a funeral, I only doubt that I would experience the same reaction as she. Inevitably I would find myself trying to mourn more picturesquely.

This kind of response to public notice is part of my attempt at the unification of my personality. I avoid using the word integrity because there is nothing particularly moral about this endeavour, it is merely something I wish to accomplish. I am saddened when anyone does not recognize that this is my aim.

Occasionally after a performance, I receive a letter from a member of the audience asking me to interpret in terms personal to her some general statement that I have made during the show (and there are many). This I do gladly but my answer often provokes another letter complaining, 'But these are the responses that you would make from the stage.' This comment makes it appallingly obvious that my correspondent has supposed that what I said in the theatre I did not mean. While it is true that I seek to entertain with every word I utter, I am never insincere. Indeed, if there is any enjoyment in *An Evening with Quentin Crisp*, it seems to me to lie in the fact that I am saying exactly what I think and that my ideas strike the audience as bizarre. A discrepancy of modes of thought is at the heart of one kind of humour. For me every performance is a small essay in self-revelation. At the end of it, whoever is seated in front of me knows me as well as people whom I have met on and off throughout the years. On occasion someone will say slightly contemptuously, 'Yes. You know all these people but are they really your friends?' I do not grade my acquaintances in order of intimacy. The ones I see most are usually those who live nearest or who make the most insistent demands. If being in love involves laying bare one's body and soul to one person, then I am in love with the world and my whole life is a slow and often interrupted wooing of the human race.

I am seen and heard therefore I am. The more often and the more clearly I am seen and heard, the more fully I feel that I am alive.

Should these sentiments reveal me to be a shallow character, I accept the criticism without a murmur.

People repeatedly warn me that, if I am not careful, I shall start to believe my own publicity. It is my opinion that I must believe it. Any other attitude would be deceitful. It would imply that lesser mortals might be dazzled by the flak with which public figures are surrounded but that we are sitting at the heart of it indifferent or, worse, cynically amused by a hoax being practised in our name upon an innocent public. We must either insist that what is printed on the dust jackets of our books or in our programme notes be reduced to human proportions or we must continually strive to become what our public relations experts claim that we are.

To be identified with our publicity is simply yet another way of merging our outward and inward selves.

Nine

Before I could justifiably be taken any further abroad, I had to consolidate my position in England. This process began in Hampstead.

There is a large hospital in the north of London called New End. (To which particular extremity of the human frame renewal is promised has never been revealed.) In a small side street running downhill beside this building stands a tiny theatre. It looks like a Protestant church in a Swiss village but it was once the hospital's mortuary. It has now been christened the New End Theatre. Thus, in my opinion, an opportunity was lost; it should have been named the Mortuary Theatre. There, night after night, a different person, preferably a celebrity, should have been placed supine under a sheet on a marble slab in the middle of the floor waiting to be asked questions, scalpel-sharp, by the audience.

At the New End I was not to give lunch-time performances and my agent decided that in an eight o'clock show, audiences must be given more. I saw the logic of this decision. However wonderful certain midday plays may be, there is no doubt that at that informal hour, people will accept a lower standard.

An evening at the theatre is an outing – a treat. A man chooses a day and books in advance which gives him time to practise looking eager. He washes and finds a girl to accompany him so as to spread the load of guilt that attends all wanton pursuit of pleasure. After such elaborate preparations an hour's entertainment will not do. As a way of extending the show to fill a whole evening, my agent hit on the idea of having me tell the audience just before the interval that it would be given pieces of paper on which it could write questions. These, in the second half of the evening, I would endeavour to answer. The programme was now divided into two more or less equal parts and lasted in all about two-and-a-quarter hours. This scheme worked like magic. It is very difficult for an amateur like me to cajole strangers into asking questions. I do not possess that ample lovability which enabled comedians to persuade music-hall audiences to sing and it must be remembered that what I was asking would put a greater strain on people's nerves. You sing in chorus: asking questions is a solo performance. The anonymity of the written word made everybody bolder – even me. I was replying to a sea of faces not to one threatening or defenceless individual. Even on a bad night when only two or three slips of paper were handed to me after the interval, audiences realized from the answers that I gave that whatever the question I would take it seriously and treat it with sympathy. Finding that no one had to be profound or witty made everybody bolder. They talked; sometimes they even shouted each other down.

This device of the written questions was not only useful to anyone in the theatre who wished to communicate with me, it also helped me to make a long overdue connection with the world.

Someone once said to me, 'I wonder what your material would be like if delivered by a real actor.' Somewhat shaken I asked what the question meant. I was told that it was obvious that everything I said was written on the inside of my skull and that I was merely reading it. I know that I have never quite eliminated this monotonous element from the first half of the show because even in America a critic said the same thing in a milder form. He remarked that he preferred the second half of the programme because then the colour returned to my voice. From answering the questions, at first blandly but in later shows as though I were speaking to one person, I am gradually learning to address a whole group of listeners as though it was one person. This I take to be part of the performer's craft.

While I was in Hampstead, I was asked no hostile questions but I did receive one amusing but angry letter. A married woman with children wrote to tell me that I was an idol with feet of clay up to my armpits. She was incensed because I had said that marriage and motherhood were impediments to style. I replied apologizing for having annoyed her. On stage or off, it is occasionally my intention to tease but never to offend. She forgave me.

Not long after I had left the New End Theatre, it was sold. In an interview with the press its owner stated that my two weeks there were the only time she had ever made money. It is only fair to say that this happy though short-lived result was not due to any superiority of my performances over others given at the New End. It happened solely because I required no expenditure of time or cash on rehearsals, scenery or direction.

Except at festivals, this two-part format is the one in which my programme has remained ever since.

You know when you have succeeded in the eyes of other actors: they send you telegrams. This did not happen to me until I went to the Duke of York's Theatre. It is in what is called the West End, that ill-defined area of London which includes Shaftesbury Avenue, the Strand and a few dim streets between. Towards this mysterious region the tired eyes of provincial leading ladies are forever turned as the three sisters looked towards Moscow. I took my graduation to St Martin's Lane calmly not because I am by nature blasé but because I am not an actor. Dearly as I would love to see the process of movie-making from the inside, it is obvious that I could only lend my gracious presence to a film as certain other notorious characters have done. I could never play a part. Who could I pretend to be? Nevertheless many of my friends very kindly decided to treat my arrival in the West End as the ascent of a theatrical Mount Everest.

In reality I was a stop-gap.

A thriller had been playing at the Duke of

York's Theatre which, although it had been running only a few weeks and in spite of the presence of Miss Phillips in the cast, had failed so utterly that the management had decided to take it off. While I was totally on the outside of show business, I never gave a thought to the magnitude of a disaster of this kind. Apparently even a small theatre in London costs £2,500 a week empty. Running a group of them must be like letting rooms on a desperate scale. Managements never know when a part of their kingdom may suddenly become vacant. When this happens, a mad dash must instantly be made to find something – anything – that will in some measure lighten the terrible financial burden. This was the situation that brought me face to face with Brian Rix. After all those bedroom farces at the Whitehall Theatre I hardly recognized him with his trousers up.

In his watch-tower, Mr Jackson noticed that the lights had gone out at the southern end of St Martin's Lane. Immediately he rushed me to the scene of the accident. Mr Rix agreed to see me, the reason again being that my act required so little preparation. Even my lighting arrangements only took a few minutes to settle. If it had been necessary, I could have gone on the stage the evening of the day we met.

'How many people a day did you speak to in Edinburgh?' Mr Rix asked as we stood in the empty theatre.

'About two hundred and fifty,' I replied.

Mr Rix seemed relieved. 'What's the first thing that you say to them?'

I explained that I used to tell the audience that I was about to deliver a straight talk from a bent speaker but that someone had objected to this opening on the ground that it gave homosexuality a bad name.

'What do you say now?'

'I say that I have been forbidden to say that this is a straight talk from a bent speaker.'

I got the job.

Once again mere chance had come to my aid and placed me in what might at least be called the fourth division of the game I longed to play. I was being assisted not merely by the particular misfortune that had befallen Mr Rix but in a general way by the decade in which this had occurred. Before the invention of the Edinburgh Festival with its fringe down to its toes, I would never have been allowed into any theatre to do nothing but stand before a paying audience and say what I thought.

The Duke of York's is what an actor would call a small theatre but to me it was big. I could no longer chat. I was compelled in some measure to declaim.

If such a thing is possible, I was becoming more theatrical.

After my initial performance in the West End, I and half the audience went to a party given by Olga Deterding, as far as I know, my only millionairess. We assembled in her penthouse at the corner of Clarges Street and Piccadilly. I had been introduced to her some months before and so was less surprised than some of my acquaintances by the opulent jokiness of our hostess's home.

The main room contained a dummy man appearing perpetually to be urinating in a corner, a stuffed sheep, innumerable science fiction burglar alarms and a sports commentator's clock on which tenths of seconds ran by like demi-semi-quavers. The apartment was large but part of the ceiling was so low that one evening I saw a very tall man charge through the room with his head bent forward like that of a Spanish bull until he came to an area where he could stand upright.

Through this oddly appointed space, from the roof above to the floor below, ran a spiral staircase. I never ventured upwards but frequently went downwards because that was where the food was served. I once spent an evening with Miss Deterding when there was only one other guest. A magazine, which I think was called *People*, had asked her to write something for it. She had decided on me as her subject. Since she did not need the fee, she must have decided to do this purely for my sake. I do not think this article was ever completed but she interviewed me absolutely seriously and covered a lot of sheets of paper with notes. On all the other occasions when I was with her the place was full of guests – chiefly Indian princesses of spectacular beauty.

It is always possible for anyone to judge the financial status of his host by the distance of the table tops and chair seats from the floor. The higher the income bracket, the lower the furniture.

In Miss Deterding's home all horizontal surfaces were well below the knee.

The rooms looked neither carefully planned nor haphazard. It was as though the décor were the result of a system of taste to which the key had been lost. I have no idea whether or not Miss Deterding's places of abode in other capital cities were like the one in London but if she felt herself to be represented by the look of the apartment in Clarges Street, it is impossible to tell what she wanted the world to think of her. In a way this was appropriate. She was a veiled character – a restless woman who often gave the impression that people were on the verge of irritating her. To me she was unfailingly kind though I was never given the faintest idea why.

One of her problems was that she seemed to think of the press as a door through which she might enter a world even wider than the one she already occupied. She was strangely reluctant to be photographed but constantly invited journalists to her home although she seldom liked what was written about her. For that she could not be blamed. Fleet Street frequently made her out to be an absolute fool. Once a paper printed the story that she had written to the Queen to make sure that a party she, Miss Deterding, was giving would not clash with some royal occasion. She could not shrug off her resentment at being made to seem so unsophisticated. My fingers will not type the words 'her money became a burden to her' but I do think that her wealth was like a lazy servant – better than nothing but a source of unremitting annoyance because it never fulfilled her most urgent needs. Certain people seemed to treat her badly simply because she was rich. At one gathering a guest arrived with five of his friends none of whom Miss Deterding knew. When she protested, his reply was, 'You can afford it.' The poor escape such rudeness as this.

It is bad enough to suspect that you are loved for your wealth alone; to discover that, because of it, you are openly despised is too much.

I cannot say that I ever expected to become a close friend of Miss Deterding but when she died I was sorry.

When I was transferred to the Ambassador's Theatre, another change overtook the show. Because of the shape of the auditorium there, it was decided that I should arrive on stage from the wings. I was being seduced by fate into observing the normal traditions of the theatre. As I stood behind the backdrop waiting to go on, inevitably I started to rev up my engine. I shut my eyes so that when I opened them on stage they would be wet and dark. I held my hands high above my head so that when they were first seen they would be pale and the veins would be countersunk. Most important of all, I started to breathe deeply. At every inhalation I lowered my diaphragm until it almost touched my pelvic bone. I have no idea if real actors go in for these antics, I merely found myself practising them. The body of the performance changed little: only the beginning and the end were altered; they became less naturalistic. Originally, just as I had begun by asking the doorman if it was time to start, so I concluded by looking at my watch and saying we should stop. In other words at first everything was done to lower the expectations of audiences. Now I was trying to live up to what they had a right to see.

For my increased theatricality I was to pay a terrible price.

While I only worked in festivals or at lunch-time my humble station in life saved me from the sansculottes of the profession. As soon as I appeared in St Martin's Lane, a deputation from Equity, waving its tattered banners, marched on the Duke of York's Theatre to ask the management why it was employing someone who was not a member of the union. Mr Rix, never completely at a loss, explained that I was not acting – that I was very sincere. This argument was thought to be specious so now, in one small respect, I am like the great Maxine Sullivan. At a public meeting in New York, I once heard her say, 'I know I am an actor because I have an Equity card.'

One night at the Duke of York's Theatre one of the questions asked was, 'Can't you prevent the audience from laughing too soon? I'm a little hard of hearing.' Until that moment I had tried to say every sentence as though it were a joke in itself and, at the same time, the prelude to another, bigger joke. I did this because I never knew when people were going to laugh. It now dawned on me, though dimly, that it was up to me to decide when laughter was permitted. I remembered having heard actors talk of controlling the audience and now presumed that it was of this problem that they were speaking.

A day was soon to come when I seemed to be about to learn the answer to this conundrum. Instead I learned something better.

A friend told me that Elaine Stritch wished to meet me. At the time she was rolling about on her bed in the London Clinic. As she could hardly escape, I telephoned and asked if she would like a visit from me. She said she would.

In real life, if you can call the London Clinic real life, Miss Stritch is much milder than when on television she is bringing the immaculate Mr Sinden to heel. Her voice is less of a growl and the corners of her mouth are less sharp. Though in no way coy, she is very feminine.

I realized that our meeting was the opportunity that might never come again to ask an undeniable expert what was meant by this to me mysterious notion of audience control. 'Don't bother with any of that, honey,' she said. 'Just get 'em to like you.'

Since that unforgettable afternoon, I have tried to make what historians will one day call 'Stritch's First Law' the guiding principle of my life.

I can't say that I have always succeeded.

While I was in the West End, I received an even angrier letter of complaint than the one sent to me by the Hampstead housewife. A man who ruled an orchestra in Brighton or, perhaps, Bournemouth wrote to say that he did not consider a lot of philosophizing based on shaky premises was entertainment. I replied at once with an apology and a cheque for the price of admission that he so bitterly regretted having paid. Unlike the Hampstead lady, he did not acknowledge my effort to make amends.

Speaking more generally, I could not help becoming aware how deeply disappointed in the show were certain members of London's gay community. They could not get it into their heads that I am not someone who hires halls throughout the land in order to deliver a manifesto. I myself am hired by Mr Rix or others to bring people into the theatre by whatever means I can. I never mention homosexuality unless, in the second half of the programme, I am asked about it. Even then I do not dwell on the subject because I fear that it may not be one that many members of the audience wish to discuss. In thinking this I am justified. Once a woman asked me a question about Lesbianism. I replied; she replied; I replied. At that point a man's voice cried out, 'Can't we move on to something of more general interest?'

During an interval at one theatre, while as usual I was autographing books in the auditorium, a young man bounced forward and in an accusatory tone said, 'You're reading from a script.' When I denied this, he barked, 'Yes, you are.' I modified my negative by explaining that though at that time there had never been a speech written down, tested for length and then memorized, I was making use of a certain amount of the text of *How to Have a Life Style* – one of the books that I was at that very moment signing. My accuser was dissatisfied with this reply.

'There are a lot of gay people here tonight,' he

said, 'and we're waiting for you to tell the audience you're gay.'

I was unable to suppress my amusement. 'How could that possibly be necessary?' I asked. 'What do you think brings people here except that I am the subject of *The Naked Civil Servant*?'

'All the same, that's what we want,' the young man persisted. I suggested that he should write down a question that would elicit from me my guilty secret.

When I unfolded what I took to be his question, it said, 'Are you an active or a passive homosexual or are you just acting?' I replied that if by acting he meant pretending to be somebody else, then acting I was not. I further explained that by temperament I was a passive human being but that, if the writer of the question was curious about my sexual techniques, he could rest assured that in a very long lifetime I had probably done everything that he could imagine. It is my secret opinion that even among heterosexuals, in a prolonged relationship both (or all) parties try all the permutations of which their nervous systems and the limitations of their anatomies are capable. To my mind all attempts to relate sexual habits to temperament are doomed. Secretly I could not help reflecting sadly on the fact that now, when at last the straight people of the world are willing to drop the subject of my long dead sex life, gay people cannot leave it alone.

All in all I worked for seven weeks in one part or another of the Cooney Marsh empire. When I left, the stage door-keeper said, 'You will come back,

won't you? You could be a one man *Mouse Trap*.'
In spite of my indifference to the venues that I
work in, this experience apparently changed me.
After it, somebody commented, 'You've – um – er
– expanded.'

One of the rewards of performing in a more
central locality was that such wonderful people
came round to my dressing-room after the show.

One such was Harold Pinter. I was introduced
to him more than ten years ago. Someone who then
lived in the same house as I and who had known
Mr Pinter before there was such a person sent him
a copy of my autobiography drawing his attention
to the page on which his fair name was mentioned.
This led to a visit from Mr Pinter to our house to
meet old friends whom he had known when he was
a touring actor. At that time I was making feeble
efforts to become state-owned with the help of the
Arts Council. Mr Pinter offered to recommend me
for a grant. Some time later he invited me to a party
in the days when he still lived in Hanover Terrace
and I mean terrace. That is to say that it is
impossible to reach the door of Number Seven
without going back to Number One and walking
along the piazza. While I stood in front of the
playwright's house, before I could ring the bell, the
mottled glass door was opened by a man in a white
coat. I was dazzled by the splendour of the way in
which successful dramatists live. If, as critics at that
time asserted, playwrights were preoccupied with
their kitchen sinks, they must have been of solid
gold. At that party, half the guests seemed to be
actresses and the other half their agents. In the

room where all these illustrious people fore-gathered, I noticed that a copy of my book had been left with kindly negligence on a table where all might see it.

Because he is so dark, his eyes not emphasized but in some way hidden by his glasses, and because he introduces into his real-life dialogue the same long silences that are employed in his plays, Mr Pinter presents to the world a brooding, almost stern aspect. With few facial movements and no gestures of the hands, he gives an impression of stillness and great density of character. It is possible to imagine situations in which he would be absolutely, even unreasonably, implacable but to me he has always been more than polite. He has been actively kind – motivated, I think, by a muted chivalry towards the weak.

After hearing me at the Duke of York's Theatre, Mr Pinter took Lady Antonia Fraser, two other guests and me to supper. When someone remarked that at last the world seemed to have accepted me, our host added 'And about time too.' With the minimum of direct praise, which can only embar-rass, he remembers always to convey to those about him that he is on their side.

Another remark, which I now weave into the show whenever possible, was made on that evening. I was asked what I had thought of my first fleeting glimpse of New York. I explained that the only possible sorrow that an Englishman could feel about such a visit was the realization that the British could live on the food thrown away every dawn in that city. Antonia Fraser's suggestion was:

'They give you doggy bags. What we need now is a doggy Concorde.'

On another evening, when a famous actress accompanied by a friend arrived in my dressing-room, it was stuffed with strange art students. I was compelled to apologize for not offering introductions; I couldn't remember any of their names. The students said, 'I am Mary, I am Tom,' and so on. The new visitor replied, 'I am Claire and this is Philip' – an example to my mind of true graciousness. They were Miss Bloom and Mr Roth.

When my reign at the Ambassador's Theatre ended, I would have been at a loose end had it not been for the proprietor of that very café where a few years ago I had met the man from Granada Television who had introduced me to Mr Mitchell. This establishment was christened the As-You-Like-It coffee bar but as none of its habitués had the stamina to utter seven words in a row, it came to be called 'The As'.

Unlike his customers, the man who ran the place was blessed with boundless energy and un-quenchable optimism and he was mad about the theatre. From time to time he would leave a hooligan in charge of the premises and rush with a taxi full of tea, coffee and sandwiches to various stage doors. This operation required split-second timing. If the tea arrived too soon, it might cool before the player who had ordered it left the stage; if it arrived late, he might not have time to sip it before his next cue. All the habitués of the café knew that they must neither move nor speak while the food and drink was being packed by the owner whose lips could be seen moving silently as he memorized what was for whom. The absence of speech and the staccato movements made these occasions like silent films. For me, as for many, visiting The As was a leisure occupation. I never minded waiting to pay my bill until the proprietor returned from the Adelphi or the Vaudeville. I welcomed delays as I had only gone to the place to pass the time.

When not flying round the West End like a blue bottle in a third-class railway carriage or ministering to his part-time residents, the owner telephoned various producers and casting directors to recommend unknown singers and dancers. Of these aspirants he spoke in terms so glowing as to be a source of entertainment to the diners who listened shamelessly to these conversations and occasionally tried to take part in them.

This indefatigable gentleman trafficked in souls with exactly the same eagerness that he lavished upon the sale of food. Tea was delicious, Florentine biscuits were divine and when he spoke over the telephone about any of his protégés, they sang like Caruso and, as dancers, were Mr Astaire's only rivals. Little did I guess that I would one day be on this sumptuous menu. With what hyperboles he recommended me to provincial theatre owners I dared not think but he seemed to have little difficulty in finding engagements for me and in the most unlikely places – Bury St Edmunds, Chipping Norton, Mold. When not out of England, I happily worked for him.

Ten

The first finger that beckoned me across the Atlantic was not American but Canadian. A woman's voice spoke to me over the telephone.

'Will you come to Toronto?' she asked coolly.

'When?'

'Well, now, actually.'

'For how long?'

'Just for the day.'

If until that moment, I had only suspected that the world had gone mad, the notion now became a certainty. In fact I was still employed by several art schools and could not leave at once. I went a fortnight later and stayed a day and a half. The journey was my first long-distance flight. It is impossible not to regard the cloudscape below you as the surface of the earth. You are not aware of any motion and feel that you are standing in a disused lighthouse surveying a snowbound planet, long since bereft of human habitation, making its last meaningless, million-year dash towards the sun.

Inside the plane a cosier atmosphere prevails. The staff of British Airways has been schooled in more than mere airworthiness. The stewards address you by your name and, if you seem reluctant to eat or uncertain what to choose, with twinkling eyes and seductive smiles, they act out the various delicacies on their trolleys. Because I was such a novice, I could not help contrasting their treatment of me with that inflicted on me by the slaves of British Rail.

In other respects, I found air travel less exciting than the movies had led me to expect. No one became hysterical, no one near me was handcuffed to anyone else and I couldn't glance nervously at the ice forming on the wings because I couldn't *see* the wings. You eat, you sleep and you go to the movies. You're hardly any better off than on earth.

A tailor would say that the east coast of the new world had been poorly finished off. Coming into Canada it is hard to say at what exact moment you leave the ocean and are flying over land. At first there are below you innumerable capes, inlets, islands and tiny lakes.

Toronto is very beautiful. Its skyscrapers are honey-coloured which, as they are mostly banks, is appropriate. They seem almost to rise out of the lake and are lit horizontally by a light emanating from the water. In the middle of the city is a secular minaret which I was told was the highest free-standing structure in the world. I did not ascend it; the lifts were loaded with tourists because the day I was there was Columbus Day. This I thought was an apt coincidence because my sense of wonder at the new world compels me to go on about it as though no one had ever been there except me and Chris.

Many of the buildings in Toronto are made of identity parade glass. I hope that from the inside of these edifices you can see out. From without all I saw was a reflection of myself standing at a window with the words 'Toronto Hotel' written backwards above my head. On my first evening I had difficulty in forcing myself to stand near the window because of its immense distance from the street below.

The main purpose of my visit to Canada was to be seen and heard talking about *The Naked Civil Servant* which had recently been shown there.

It had been solicitously decided that I could not travel three thousand miles and be interviewed on the same day. In fact I could have done so without any feeling whatsoever of exhaustion. There is no such thing as jet-lag – especially if you are journeying from east to west. All the plane has to do is to go up into the air and, like Nijinsky, pause there a little; Canada will come by presently.

Appropriately the man sent to meet me when I arrived in the new world was called Mr Dvorak. In a purring limousine he escorted me to the hotel from which he promised to collect me the following evening.

Before I had fully unpacked, I received a telephone call from the Toronto office of my paperback publisher. It was the caller's intention to whisk me the following morning in and out of various radio stations. My arrival twenty-four hours early had not been in vain.

A year before, I would have been amazed at this proposal: now I remained calm. I had learned in the meantime the difference between hardback and paperback publishing.

Hardback publishers are not seriously in the business of selling their wares; they are content with laying them at the reader's feet. Any more energetic practice might seem ungentlemanly. At parties in the last few years I have met men in the trade who could be bullied into agreeing with this statement so long as their names were never mentioned in this connection. They admit that there are no junior employees in their offices whose function day after day is to read the papers in the hope of finding that one of the firm's authors is dead, has been sent to prison or done anything else to merit a reprint. To laymen it is obvious that televiewers love to see writers in alpaca suits sitting on swivel chairs and talking about their sex lives provided that these divine beings do not make the mistake of rabbiting on about their dreary books. Inside the business no one can bring himself to accept that writing is not a literary career but a personality racket. Many English writers are relieved to know that their actual bodies will never be used as sales adjuncts. It might have been difficult, for instance, to persuade E. M. Forster to run round Bedford Square in a funny hat. As for me, I've got the hat – all I ask is, 'Which way do I go?'

For this reason I had been bewildered when I discovered that Cape had no intention of dipping its toe – much less plunging head first – into the tide of publicity that flowed first from Granada's and then from Thames's television programmes about me: there were to be no more printings of my autobiography in its original format. Since that terrible time, Duckworth has been kind enough to bring out a different hardback version solely in order to attract more recent reviews while Fontana, which may be another floor, another room or merely another desk in Collins, published a wonderful cheap – or, at least, cheaper – edition. They are, moreover, pleased to make use of the element of vulgarity in my nature. For this purpose they have a press office in which at least one person is constantly at work. Day and night, like a lighthouse, her gaze ransacks the ocean of human activity in search of an island (a mere rock will do) on which a bookstall can be set up. In England, wherever I went to speak to the multitude, she was willing, nay eager, to pay my fare and feed me. I was delighted to find that, though she organized these book-signing sessions with great efficiency, ruled provincial book sellers firmly and commanded area representatives to meet our trains as though we were ambassadors, she was never shrill. She remained forever silky.

As with London so with Toronto. In Canada, because of the whirlwind nature of my visit, I was taken to four small radio stations in one day. These brief interviews were much as I had expected but I had not imagined that Canadian men would be such a self-indulgent shape. There is no national face above the forty-ninth parallel but there is a typical figure. In spite of all that ice-hockey that we see on English television, I do not think much exercise is taken by the average Torontan.

Between these appointments, we managed to wedge in several large meals and a visit to a paper called the *Body Politic*. This periodical is the gay voice of Toronto. As its name implies, it is more militant than, say, *Gay News* but it is determined rather than strident. The issue of the paper I was shown espoused the cause of a man who had been dismissed from his job on the explicit grounds that he was homosexual. He was a horse trainer. It is difficult to imagine what goes on in the minds of some heterosexuals.

The *Body Politic* is run by very young people – several men and a girl. They occupy a warehouse situated beyond the business and shopping areas of the city. We went up to the editorial office in a lift like the one which Miss Dietrich fell to the bottom of in Pittsburgh. The room where we talked was large and airy – possibly difficult to heat in winter but the staff is dauntless. I was given a cup of tea and questioned about my private life. I apologized for my lack of aggression. I think it saddened them but they remained unfailingly polite.

After this interview some of those with whom I had been speaking accompanied me through the streets in search of lunch. They noticed without surprise that a few passers-by stared at me but expressed amazement that I paid no attention to any of the 'pretty boys' that wandered past us. I can only express a counter-surprise. My life has, in recent times, become literally an open book. Everyone who is interested in me at all knows that in earlier years I spent a great deal of time trying to qualify as a pretty boy. Surely they must be able to guess that, because of this, I am horribly aware how self-regarding, feeble and generally not worth the money this particular species can be.

When I left Canada, I did not immediately return to England. I went to New York. Entering the United States I proferred my passport for the very first time in my life. A gigantic airport official examined it thoroughly before giving it back to me. When I thanked him and turned to go, he bent down and, in a very quiet voice, said, 'Is it nice to be vindicated at last?'

My spies are everywhere.

When, a year afterwards, I did the one-man show in Newhaven, Washington and New York, I again went to Toronto. During my later, longer visit, my impression of the city was different though not necessarily any more accurate. Mr Muggeridge, whose voice was made for expressing bland contempt, says that I live a 'show biz' life and shall never see places as they really are. He is absolutely right. The second time round everything seemed less frighteningly grand. I do not wish to imply that, during one short year, the glory of Canada had faded. All that happened was that I inhabited a slightly cheaper part of town. I do not think I even so much as walked past the Toronto Hotel where I had spent two nights of deep-piled opulence nor did I catch even a glimpse of that strange edifice that claimed to be of unparalleled height. I stayed at the Waldorf-Astoria which, contrary to what its hyphenated name might lead guests to suppose, was quite unpretentious and in no way intimidating even to someone as pathologically terrified of hotel staff as I am.

I appeared at the Workshop Theatre to which I travelled by taxi but only to show that I could. If compelled by fate to traverse the distance on foot, the journey took less than a quarter of an hour so I saw little of the city. As always, when not in my hotel room or on stage, I made sorties to various television and radio stations. Canadians are very conscious of the power of publicity. In fourteen days I was interviewed twenty-one times. In between these professional activities, I just managed visits to my two spies in Canada.

One of these was the woman who, in England twenty long, dark years before, had ruled the display firm where I had painted the faces of four thousand dolls. Now, in quieter mood, she runs a curiosity shop for cat worshippers. I am happy to say that the place harbours no actual animals but it is full of feline fetishes – cards, calendars, knick-knacks.

The other spy is the woman to whom, when she lived in Crouch End, we tried to bring notoriety by writing television plays in her name. She has now abandoned her quest for fame and settled for mere happiness. One of her daughters took me to see a dancing class. The hunger for culture is far less self-wounding in Canada than in Australia but it is present nonetheless. When I asked this girl if she was a pupil at the school, she replied that she was not – that she was a member of a ballet company. This seemed to be an improvement until I learned that she received no wages. I was saddened by hearing this. To an outsider, Canada looks physically so open, so full of light and spiritually so free from deviousness or pretence but even there there seems to be a certain amount of double thinking and therefore perhaps, though I personally saw none, of double dealing. The fact that young people donate their energies and their talents so eagerly is no argument for accepting them without payment. No art should be subsidized either by governments or, worse, by its practitioners.

Now that I habitually travel distances so much greater than formerly I would have dared or could have afforded, I am often reunited with people whom I have not seen for huge stretches of time. The changes that the years have wrought in them are consequently more obvious. So far these confrontations with the past have always given me pleasure. My friends usually seem to have grown calmer. This is a development that I applaud but, as a devotee of relativity, I must constantly remind myself that, if this is the alteration I see in them, they must find me more feverish – a suspicion recently turned into conviction by a letter received from a friend in France. It contained this warning: 'Try not to start wanting things.' It would appear that the asceticism for which I have had a life-long reputation was prompted by circumstantial necessity rather than innate spirituality. I doubt that I shall ever want things, but, now that I am free, there is no limit to my appetite for events and people.

Eleven

For weeks there were rumours that, like other wrongdoers before me, I would be sent to Australia. I tried not to hear them. Thus I did not know that this mad scheme had become a certainty until I was sitting at a lunch table opposite a Mr Cook – perhaps a descendant of that seafaring gentleman who discovered the place. In his native land he is called an entrepreneur. This I found strange. Even in England, twelve thousand miles from that proverbially no-nonsense continent, the word sounds a trifle fancy but impresario is not much better and the American word promoter carries with it a faint suspicion of chicanery. But what's in a name? He had chosen a profession in pursuit of which he travelled all over the world in search of entertainment that he could transplant in the Antipodes. While he was in America on one of these foraging sorties, he spoke with the Mr Taylor who later brought Mr Brynner in *The King and I* to England. Mr Taylor had seen me at the Duke of York's Theatre and advised Mr Cook to do the same. What chance had caused these two gentlemen to meet I never asked.

By this time I accepted that fate was my agent.

All the same, when I saw that a visit to Australia was irrevocable, I was very frightened. I explained that I had never spoken to more than seven hundred people at any one time and that even that number had proved too many. Mr Cook said that I need have no fear – that I would be wired for sound. I pointed out that Australians despise the English nation in general and would find me particularly revolting. Mr Cook said that a theatre audience was the same the whole world over and that, if I'd managed all right here, I would have no trouble there. Every objection that I raised was overruled, every doubt silenced. During this dialogue the enigmatic Mr Taylor arrived and remarked that my act would have to be made more elegant. He also suggested that its contents should be altered slightly to appeal to Australian tastes. I bowed my head assuming that he was an authority on that distant world of which I knew nothing. It transpired later that he had never been near the place.

In spite of all this reassurance, all this friendly advice, I still had secret misgivings. I was right.

The Australian tour was a disaster.

Even so, it might have been worse had not my agent succeeded in bamboozling into coming with me the young woman who had assisted me at the Duke of York's Theatre. She was of high-degree, her father being a baronet or worse, but asked why she worked when she could so easily have stayed in bed all day polishing her coronet, she replied that she needed the money. Nevertheless public relations was an odd career for her to have chosen. It is a ruthless profession whose practitioners are sometimes driven to manipulate their victims while pretending to protect them and in which fulsome praise is forever trembling on the brink of downright untruth. My assistant was a moralist and consequently spent most of her working life in a state of collapse.

She turned out to be the ideal travelling companion. Being so slight as to be hardly visible to the naked eye, she could easily be folded and stowed away in any make of car without the least inconvenience to other passengers. Moreover she not only took up very little space but also demanded almost no attention. As she did not like the real world, she spent most of her time in it asleep. Miraculously being frail turned out not to be the same thing as being scatter-brained; at least we never arrived at the wrong place on the wrong day.

As we stepped out of the plane in Sydney I reassured my companion that, it being only seven in the morning, we would easily be able to slip into our hotel unnoticed. Never was prophecy more spectacularly unfulfilled. The moment that we wheeled our luggage out of the airport, we found ourselves in a lightning storm of flash bulbs, a thunder clap of interrogation. Even when the car that was taking us to our hotel drew away from the kerb, reporters ran beside it, their lips still moving. Once we were in our rooms, the hubbub that I had assumed would cease became worse. We discovered that a small documentary movie was to be made of our arrival. There were people photographing the people photographing us. It was as though we had come to save the whole continent.

Just as the entire world adores France but has recently come to dislike the French, so, though Australians despise the British, they love England and for a while, at any rate to the press, I became the embodiment of the traditions of my native land although in fact I have always rebelled against them.

What is at the heart of this inordinate passion for Britain? I think I may by accident have hit upon the answer.

Many long, dark years ago, I took a friend to see a movie called *King Kong* (the first time round) During a dramatic episode in which a certain Miss Wray lay gibbering across Mr Kong's wrist, my companion, in a voice shrill with irritation, cried out, 'I can't think what he sees in her.' I suggested that it might be her littleness that was her attraction. Perhaps it is a similar discrepancy of sizes that binds Australia to England.

In the ten weeks that I worked for Mr Cook, I went to Orange, to Newcastle and, except for Darwin, to every capital city in his kingdom. Some of these towns I visited more than once, going there first to say that I was going there and later to do the show. In all that time I was embroiled in only one hostile interview. This was with a man and woman who were quite unable to take their minds off what I looked like. As I was leaving, the man assayed a mild send-up by remarking that, if I wished to add a few small touches to my appearance, the make-up department would be only too willing to help. In the theatre I was compelled to read no more than a dozen questions calculated to embarrass me. The word 'poof' was only used once -- at least in my hearing.

Most of the questions asked by the professional interviewers were self-deprecating. One reporter kept saying, 'We're so far from everywhere, aren't we?' I pointed out that Sydney is no further from New York than New York from Sydney. 'Well, no,' the lady grudgingly admitted.

'Nobody,' I remarked, 'is sitting by his window in America sighing because he is so far from Australia.'

'Exactly. That's just what I mean.'

'Then,' I suggested, 'remoteness is in the heart.' The young woman wrote these observations down but she didn't look as though she believed me.

Another often repeated question was, 'Australia is a cultural desert, don't you think?' This statement was wasted on me. If I ever use the word 'culture', it is to describe television programmes so boring they cannot be classed as entertainment.

Australians are a nation of Madam Butterflies. They are forever standing on the shore watching for that wisp of Heaven-knows-what that will appear on the horizon one fine day.

But why? They lack nothing. The streets beneath their feet are paved with opals. The air about them sparkles like diamonds. The atmosphere is so clear that the roofs of their houses are always as red as the day they were tiled; the walls as white as when they were first painted.

Strangers kept saying that it was a pity that we had arrived in winter but, in fact, every day that we were there was warmer than an English May. This appearance of eternal summer was reinforced by the look of the trees most of which are evergreen. Those that are look not as though their foliage had sprung spontaneously from their boughs but rather as if it had been flung on to their branches from a distance – wet. Those that are not evergreen display scarlet flowers the size of table mats.

Partly because of this halcyon weather, all Australian cities are holiday resorts. On their free days, the natives take off their socks and shoes and walk down to the sea's edge. If you tried that in London, you would feel very ill by the time you got there.

Furthermore, in Australia there seems to be no poverty. The trains are empty but the aeroplanes are full – chiefly of men carrying their board meeting suits in plastic bags. Occasionally in Sydney I saw sun-burnt old men who looked as though they were left over cold from a gold rush but there were no beggars, no street bands, no little old ladies slumped in doorways under several overcoats. Except for the black swans of Perth, there were very few even of nature's born cadgers, the birds.

I constantly tried to reassure my interviewers; I seldom succeeded. It is possible that Australians are self-deprecatory out of politeness. They may well feel that it would be graceless to flaunt their ocean-to-ocean prosperity before the hollow eyes of travellers from a dying star.

My tour of the Antipodes failed not because of any hostility from my audiences. No empty beer cans were thrown on to the stage. I foundered (and this we had not in our arrogance thought possible) on their indifference. When I strolled about the streets or went into the shops of King's Cross, the district of Sydney in which our hotel was situated, my presence seemed to be taken completely for granted.

In Melbourne the reaction was the same. I stood in the entrance to a cinema waiting for a taxi while near at hand two young men discussed whether they had or had not seen me on television a few days earlier. When they decided that they had, one of them approached and shook my hand. After the usual exchange of pleasantries, he said, 'So you're homosexual. Big deal.' I did not think these words were meant to discomfit me but rather that they were a comment on the folly of the sex-obsessed world. The same cool attitude was expressed even in Brisbane which, in other parts of Australia, is the butt of jokes similar to those that in England are heaped upon Wigan. One evening I was standing in my hotel room looking down on to one of those doll's-house churches that nestle among the skyscrapers of Brisbane when the telephone bell rang. My caller explained that he was attending a school in which his class had been told to write an essay about the television documentary programme showing my arrival in Australia. This piece of information by itself astounded me. In England no teacher would set his pupils such an inflammatory subject unless he were more interested in publicity than in a steady job. More amazing, however, than the shadowy figure of this broad-minded master was the very real student. Apparently without any prompting from his elders, he had nagged his sister into driving him into town so that he might embellish his thesis with details gathered first-hand from me. He was fourteen at the oldest yet Mr Darwin setting out in *The Beagle* cannot have had to summon up more scientific detachment than this child.

I realized instantly that I must not figure in a fifth-form essay beginning, 'When I talked with Mr Crisp in his hotel bedroom . . .' I therefore asked my visitor to accompany me to my dressing-room at the theatre where I was to perform in an hour's time. Backstage I answered all the young man's questions, without, I hope, saying anything that, if quoted, would alarm his father or his headmaster.

Even so our conversation was by no means bland. 'My friends say that you're a slob,' the boy remarked with no apparent hostility. He had noticed that my shirt was held together with a safety pin. Had he known it, this was a good night. Sometimes I seem to be dressed in chain mail.

This young man seemed critical but in no way hysterical or angry. He appeared interested in me but not unduly curious about my sex life. How different was this urbane attitude from the mixture of rudeness and cowardice that marks the behaviour of English schoolboys who on railway platforms call my name but, when I turn towards them, scamper into the nearest waiting room!

The sophistication of Australia was so complete that it did more than set the people free to come and see me; they felt sufficiently liberated to stay away.

The blame for the disasters in one's life must always fall upon oneself. I should have protested longer or louder that I could not fill a large theat e in Australia or anywhere else. I should have forced Mr Cook to believe me. There is a sense in which I betrayed him but, in spite of the staggering financial loss that he must have sustained on my account, he remained unfailingly courteous. I hope that for my part I made it clear how grateful I was for the opportunity he gave me to visit this strange continent – sparse but wealthy, barbaric but modern, self-effacing but friendly.

I felt my shame less keenly than I might have done because, to me, all performances elsewhere in the world are but dress rehearsals for America.

America

Until I went to St Andrews University in 1975, I had never left England. Before 1977 I had never been outside the British Isles. Now, only two crowded years later, I have been to every region of the earth where Crisperanto is understood except South Africa which I have never visited because I reckon they are in enough trouble there already.

Even so, I am not an experienced traveller. I never shall be because I so seldom make long voyages alone. The harrowing complexities of airports are usually faced by other people on my behalf. The person who most often shoulders this burden is my agent. When I go to the United States he makes the trip partly on his own account, seeing America as a bookshelf three thousand miles wide, but mostly he does so for my sake. I am very grateful. Being my companion in a strange land demands a certain moral fortitude. Wherever we go, people say, looking him slowly up and down, 'Ah yes. You're Quentin's personal manager.' It might mean anything but he remains calm and explains that he is a literary agent – not only mine but that of many other writers.

Occasionally some of my acquaintances sneer at the fact that, like little old ladies of the 1890s, I seem to need a travelling companion. They are rattled by my fecklessness or, more likely, by the condonation that my passivity receives from my employers. 'Do you like having your mind made up for you by others?' they snort. 'Don't you care that you are being treated like a dog, told when to sit and when to follow at your master's heels?' I remain unperturbed by their indignation. The treatment upon which they spit their scorn is not something I merely accept; I connive at it. It ensures that I am never to blame. To anyone whom the world has for so long tried to make feel ashamed this is a great relief. When I was a child my ineptitude was a burden to my parents and my teachers. They could not see that it was a greater burden to me. I wondered wanly if I would ever discover how to do anything well. At long last I have learned something even better – how not to do anything at all.

This pampered mode of travel serves not only my own purpose but also that of anyone who employs me. One evening during a week in Washington so unsuccessful that it quite put me off wanting to be President, I was taken by my sponsor to supper at the Watergate, no less. During the meal I said, 'But the going on the stage and the signing of the books are a pretext, are they not? Really I'm in the smiling and nodding racket.' Without a moment's hesitation he agreed that I was.

This being so, it is my duty when in the outer world never to appear worried about trying to decipher what an airport public address system is saying, never to be seen in tears because I have lost my ticket. No one must ever be provoked into saying that he saw me somewhere but that I looked so distraught that he didn't dare to speak to me. To this end I not only never travel alone, I have even abandoned my life-long habit of scorning strangers before they have had a chance to scorn me. Now, in public, like everyone else who has been on television, I wear perpetually an expression of fatuous affability.

There is a sense in which, however far I go, I shall never be a traveller at all. I shall never return home with a parrot in a cage and fantastic tales of what foreign people and places look like. It is in the very nature of my situation that I traverse the world not to see but to be seen.

My visit to America was given a curious overture.

A day came when, seeking new screens to conquer, Thames Television bought seven consecutive evenings of New York viewing time. Among the items shown was *The Naked Civil Servant*. I trust it was exhibited on a channel that required no sponsorship. I cannot imagine any manufacturer being willing to advertise his product during that tale of degradation unless the copy were to say, 'If you don't eat up your shredded wheat, you'll end up like Quentin Crisp.'

Whether or not this wild gamble turned out to be profitable for Thames I have no idea but it certainly made a difference to me. It foreshadowed the moment when my dream of America became a reality. From the moment that I heard what had happened, I never for long took my eyes from the western horizon.

For many months no invitation to visit the States was received but an American came to see me. This man was Mr Lindsay, the former mayor of New York – a position, in my estimation, only just south of God. I remembered from the invasion of Britain by GIs during the war that all Americans are good-looking. Even so I was amazed by Mr Lindsay's appearance. He is what television would call a new, improved Mr Niven.

He arrived in Beaufort Street at the head of his men – a producer whose nerves were worn down to their stumps by lack of sleep, an Italian cameraman and a lighting expert who only longed for glasses of Guinness.

Mr Lindsay and I were placed so close together that we must have looked like old time radio crooners sharing a microphone. The cameraman trudged through a heap of dirty sheets lying in the corner of my room presumably in the hope of getting far enough away from us to show that we were not embracing. My home affords so little space that, throughout the interview, he was compelled to balance his camera on his sagging collar bone. I could not help wondering if we would be seen in heaving close-up like the windscreen shots in a car chase.

I was too astonished by the entire incident to remember much of my conversation with my visitor but I do recall that he asked me if I was planning to go to the States. My reply was another question: 'What about my sin?' To reassure me, my interviewer waltzed casually through a catalogue of names belonging to famous Englishmen who had safely carried their tarnished images across the Atlantic Ocean but a moment later, perhaps fearing that he had offered too much encouragement, he was warning me that I would have to undertake not to overthrow the government by force. I issued a counter-warning but have since learned that no one who is not born in America can be President.

It seemed to me unlikely that this dialogue would ever be heard in New York but I was wrong. My spy for that city has since told me that this interview formed part of a programme called *Good Morning, America.* That means that it was seen by eleven million people with half-closed eyes. My informant also said that Mr Lindsay seemed embarrassed. The camera evidently sees more than the eye. At the time of his visit he seemed to me polite but relaxed, interested but not inquisitive. He personified that effortless sociability that I now know to be the national style of America.

If proof were needed that democracy is alive and well and living in America this entire episode would provide it.

Mr White says that an Englishman is unhappy until he has explained America; I would say that he might feel guilty if he did not praise it.

Though, at a first glance, New York is less beautiful than Toronto – less airy, less golden – to me it was more exciting because it is the city of my dreams. The moment I caught sight of it, I wanted it and stretched my arms through the car window towards the skyscrapers like a child beholding a Christmas tree. Every street along which we drove brought back the memory of some long dead movie seen when life was dreary and only the world of celluloid was rich and full. Every person on the sidewalks reminded me of the soldiers who invaded London during the happy time.

On this first visit we were the guests of Mr Bennett. This was as it should be. He is the very spirit of the place – a jumping-up-and-down man of limitless hospitality who is wild about the entertainment industry. He arranged for us to live for two-and-a-half days in a splendour to which it would be ruinous to become accustomed. In a hotel suite large enough to house a Catholic family, I was given a bed in which four people could have slept without ever being introduced. Everything in America is on wide screen.

Mr Bennett is the very model of a modern millionaire; that is to say that he dresses for all occasions like a college student. Thus attired he took me, on my last evening in New York, through various theatres of the Schubert group. There, since he invented *A Chorus Line*, he is obviously sacred. The manager of one of these houses walked solemnly before us like a mace-bearer to shoo away any ushers or ticket collectors who might mistakenly have dared to address us. Of all the snippets of entertainment that I sampled in this way the one that impressed me most was my glimpse of Mr Borge. Except that he occasionally plays a few notes on the piano, he does less on stage than I do but to so much more effect.

Finally my host took me to Sardi's. His mode of living is like that of Nature herself; he leaves a wide margin for the unexpected. Though there were only four invited guests, we sat at a table large enough for a board meeting. Within seconds this turned out to have been a wise stratagem. We were joined for a few seconds each by a series of diners from other parts of the room. Among other celebrities I was introduced to Mr von Sydow. He did not look God-ridden; he has a pink face, corn-gold hair and a handshake that could force you to your knees. Either in Mr Bergman's picture or in Sardi's, he was acting.

One man who visited our table became highly excited when he saw me. 'Oh,' he cried glancing rapidly from me to Mr Bennett and back again, 'is there going to be a collaboration of some kind?' Mr Bennett explained that this was a secret. From somewhere a quiet voice murmured, 'Then why are you in Sardi's?'

Throughout the meal – throughout every meal – because of all this darting to and fro, the waiters never enjoy a clear run from the tables to the kitchen. With their trays held high above their heads, they move, stop, start again like six o'clock traffic on Brooklyn Bridge except that there are no tantrums and no collisions.

In Sardi's there is more waving, more squeaking, more embracing than anywhere else on earth. An English restaurateur would find some way of putting a thin-lipped stop to all this hectic conviviality. If he did not, his staff would leave.

This is the very heart of the difference between the British and the American way of life. The English actually want their jobs to be boring so that they can strike. They wish their friends to be dull so that they need not feel inferior to them. New Yorkers, on the other hand, strenuously resist all tendencies to reduce people and events to their lowest common factor. Many years before I ever dreamed that I would one day visit the United States, a friend wrote to me saying, 'Over here everyone is rich and everyone is handsome.'

This is true but it is not all. My correspondent omitted to add that everyone is eager. This is to me by far the most important attribute of Americans. They want to speak, they want to listen and they will endure quite a lot of inconvenience to prevent the colour from being drained out of experience. They like people to be unusual in any way they know how. Even being foreign will do. Visiting Englishmen they adopt as pets and coo at them as though they were budgies that can nearly speak American. For the same reason they worship actors who, to civilians, are the very icons of that instant success the notion of which even the most down-trodden waif never wholly relinquishes. If a man who was once a farm boy becomes a senator, people are quietly pleased but the metamorphosis has been a lengthy, even a daunting process and no one is still around who can vividly describe those early straw-nibbling years. If, however, someone is in a soap advertisement one year and the next is playing the lead in a technicolor, wide-screen first feature, everyone – even little children – can bear witness to the miracle. In the shrivelled hearts of the English such an event, if it ever occurred, would arouse only envy but in America it would inspire hope.

On the morning of my departure from New York Mr Bennett, who had become aware of my infatuation with his native land, came to the hotel and presented me with a large American flag. All the way back to Heathrow I wore it as though it were my college scarf. Perhaps this was an act of treason. If accused, I would have pleaded invincible ignorance.

Had I died on the way home, I should have been extremely put out at the time but later, looking down from my cloud, I would have been content.

The purpose of that first visit to the Islands of the Blessed was so that Mr Bennett might cast an eye over me and my agent. He wished to buy the stage rights of *The Naked Civil Servant*. In the end, for reasons that were veiled from me, an option on my autobiography was sold to Mr Elkins, an impresario so famous that a book called *The Producer* has been written about him. When, the following year, I again crossed the Atlantic, it was in order that I might begin to work for him. The nearest I can come to describing the nature of this new employment is to mention I once said that of any event my agent would demand to know if there was any money in it but Mr Elkins would merely ask, 'How often will my name be mentioned?' With this prognosis they both agreed.

I have recently been involved in such a whirlwind courtship of the universe that I cannot now remember whether I initially met my American employer before or after my first visit to New York. I seem to have become aware of his existence gradually from oblique murmurs issuing from my agent's lips.

Like Mr Cook who took me to Australia, Mr Elkins was once an actor. When I asked him why he had become an impresario, he said that it was the only thing that he knew how to do. From this we may infer that promotion is where actors go when they die. I asked the question because indirectly I was learning what an uneasy, even hazardous, profession being an entrepreneur can become. He has to be in possession of the money, the script, the leading actor and the right theatre all on the same day.

Impresarios are frequently asked by televisionaries when some scheme or other first occurred to them. They look at the toe-cap of one expensive shoe and murmur dreamily, 'I got the basic idea in 1946.' I used to think that replies such as this were a joke. I now know they can be only too true.

It is not easy to say whether Mr Elkins enjoys going to the theatre, likes the company of stage people or is fascinated by the complexities of show business. Even if he adores all these aspects of his profession, it still does not explain why he was so keen to own *The Naked Civil Servant*. Perhaps the answer is simply that whatever he wants he wants absolutely. When I first met him he seemed to wish to make my life story into a straight play for presentation in London. Later, to my great relief, the project turned into a musical to be staged on Broadway. I remember saying that I wanted whatever he wanted. His reply was, 'In that case we shall never quarrel.' We never did but, in case I appear to be seeking praise for being self-effacing, I must add that, as my agent once pointed out, I can only afford to be so nice because he's so nasty.

That I always accepted Mr Elkins' judgement does not mean that I understood him. On the contrary, to this day he mystifies me. He is a small man whose energy is out of all proportion to his bulk like something dangerous in nuclear physics and he is made restless by ambition as another man might be wracked by indigestion. Nevertheless, in a life so peripatetic that half of it is spent in the sky, he is a family man constantly getting married, begetting children and being visited by his relatives.

His appearance is as extreme as his nature. His hair is white but his eyes are black. As if this did not make them startling enough, he opens them by lowering his lower lid rather than raising his upper lid and keeps them so wide open that he looks perpetually astonished by the enormity of his commitments.

In contrast with him his newest wife is calm and unusually gentle. Perhaps she is the heart of the hurricane.

Once I had become involved in show business, however peripherally, a question arose which I couldn't help asking myself (since I dared not interrogate the people concerned).

Why do rich men put their money into theatrical ventures?

They cannot possibly be interested in becoming even richer. If that were their aim, they would invest their spare cash in oil or automobiles or, indeed, almost anything rather than the stage.

Speaking in very general terms, I think the answer has to be that 'angels' are interested in girls. I know that, on a rainy night, a woman can be pressed into service for a few pence but, in those circumstances, a man's power over the opposite sex is seldom witnessed by his rivals. This may vitiate the sense of triumph. If, however, he allows it to be known that he finances plays, then, wherever he goes in public, all women within a radius of half a mile will creep a little closer to him and, with elaborate unconcern, will present him with their noble profiles or worse. With no effort on his part, Mr Midas can thus surround himself with girls, all of them daring, some of them beautiful and a few with talent – if anyone cares. Furthermore, at any moment (and there must be many) when the conversation in his club becomes boring, a man in these circumstances can glance at his digital watch and sigh, 'I'm afraid I simply must run along and see how my latest show is doing.' As he rises from his ragged leather chair, all eyes will turn enviously towards him, all hearts will silently ask the palpitating question, 'Does he really know Miss Christie and, if so, how well?' If wealth is thus devoted to the strengthening of an image of masculine desirability rather than squandered on Inland Revenue – that old whore who will do anything for money – few of us would think it had been unwisely spent.

Although I never met any of them, I presume it was with these strange men that Mr Elkins so feverishly dealt.

The smiling and nodding racket has many branches. Chief among these is to be interviewed by televisionaries or on radio programmes. For this purpose I went whizzing round the United States – to Boston, to Chicago (where, to my surprise, there was not a glimpse of Edward G. Robinson) and so on. Mr Warhol's first law states that it is possible to be famous for being famous. A corollary of this axiom is that you can often be interviewed simply because you are so often interviewed.

Of the two media, radio and television, I prefer the latter. Even in real life I tend to act out whatever I am saying. This habit is not only useless if no one can see me, it also lulls me into thinking that I am being more expressive than I am in audible terms. On television I feel free but I rapidly learned to conceal my enthusiasm. The technicians despised me when they realized that I was enjoying myself.

In a small way, being an interviewee is a craft. It certainly requires a technique. It is essential to bear in mind that facial movements are exaggerated by photography. If you roll your eyes, they will step out of your skull and slide across the screen. On the other hand, the microphone bevels the edges of even the most articulate voice. You must therefore keep your features calm while charging your voice with melodramatic emphasis – a little like rubbing your head and patting your stomach at the same time.

While performing this feat, you must try to remain aware which camera is watching you and also calculate how much of you it can see. If I did not think my hands were visible I tried, which isn't easy, not to move them at all. I thought that viewers might be aware that some hidden gesture was being made and might be distracted by trying to guess what it was. Even when you are sure that your hands can be seen, you have to remember to hold every gesture long enough for the camera to turn towards it and tell the world what it has seen. These seemed to me to be the chief purely mechanical problems of being interviewed.

The remaining difficulty lies in becoming aware, before your brief moment in the limelight is half over, what kind of reaction is expected of you. As I crossed the States, I became involved in every possible interpretation of my life, grave, flippant, political, psychological, religious. In the Far West, I came face to face with Mr Snyder. He is in the human document industry so remembered anguish could not be shuffled off with a jolly laugh. With Mr Cavett in New York, I was in the entertainment business. It was with him that I felt most at ease. He is working with and for his conscripted audience in the studio and he sits beside rather than opposite you. He is your straight man (comic as opposed to bent) and he obligingly feeds you questions to which he already knows the punch lines.

If your interrogator seems to have no definite method of conducting the dialogue, it may be necessary to treat the situation like a geography examination. Few of us have enough stamina to study the whole world so we trust to luck. The night before our test, we take our atlas from its shelf, blow the tell-tale dust from the top of it and open it at random. If the pages part at China, that is what we study. Of course, the next day we discover that the main question in our paper concerns France. Our answer begins, 'France is not like China.' Translated into television terms, this means that if you arrive at the studios with a wonderful anecdote about your mother and some ill-briefed clot says, 'How's your father?' you reply, 'Father's worn out coping with my mother who . . .' This would be described by a lawyer as converting public questions to private use.

Another by no means distasteful duty that I felt I owed to Mr Elkins was to be photographed as often as possible. At a party given in honour of Miss Midler at the Waldorf Hotel, I was led across the room to meet her. We shook hands and exchanged a few gracious phrases to give the photographers time to gather round us. Then, standing as close to her as I dared, I turned towards the largest camera and smiled. Very quietly Miss Midler whispered, 'That's right, baby. Do the whole bit.'

I have followed her instructions ever since.

Whenever I become aware that I am being photographed, I give myself over to the occasion as completely as I can. I stand where I am told to stand. I try to look as I am required to look. As I am not paying for the results of all this attention, it seems the least I can do. Although it may be no such thing, I behave as though anyone's desire to take a picture of me is a compliment. Doing this is a politeness exactly parallel with giving my full attention to the kind remarks of strangers. For this reason, though I play up to the camera if I am given time, were I 'snapped' unawares, I would never try to prevent an unflattering or even a ludicrous likeness of me being printed.

I am not feverishly interested in the end product. Given a picture of myself I would accept it though I would not frame it or hang it on the wall. If I am not offered a print, I do not ask for one. This attitude is probably the result of having worked in art schools for so many years. When I first took up that profession, the model's lowly station in life debarred him from walking casually about the 'life' room. I would never have been employed again in any establishment where I had made so bold as to stare critically at the drawings that were being done.

Nowadays there is no reason why models should not survey the paintings of students and even comment upon them. Democracy is here to stay. Nevertheless old-timers seldom take advantage of the new regime. Others apart from me are aware that this is so. A short while ago, just before I gave up posing in art colleges, I was resting between sessions in one room when a model from another class came and scrutinized the work in progress. After she had departed, the art master, in tones of glacial contempt, said, 'The hallmark of an amateur.'

In spite of my indifference to the end product I cannot help being aware that the earth is now passing through the second photographic age.

The first began just before or during the Great War when the box camera, the 'Brownie', brought the taking of snapshots within reach of the middle classes both financially and in terms of expertise. In that distant time, the criterion of a good photograph was simply that all the relevant subject matter was clearly recognizable. There was no nonsense about composition then. In fact, when I was young, photography was considered to be the enemy of art. Somebody once brought disgrace upon himself when he tried to show at the Royal Academy's summer exhibition a picture found by the judges to have been painted over a photographic background. Today, though it might be thought dull, this method of working would in no way be considered immoral. All students are encouraged to learn to use a camera properly firstly because carrying small reproductions of their work is so much less burdensome than carting actual canvases to art galleries and advertising agencies and secondly so as to have something from which to work when the light on a landscape changes or a model drops dead.

Today there is no opposition by art to photography. Cameras and artist's materials are equally aesthetic and equally expensive but both have become the paraphernalia of a game any number can play. Though cameras are now far more sophisticated than formerly, they have passed through the phase when they were difficult to use and emerged into the common light of day almost amateur-proof. It is no longer miraculous to be able to make a visual record of a person or an event. We have moved on to a point at which the design and the lighting of a photograph come under perpetual discussion. Perhaps the notion that aesthetic values are involved helps to justify the financial outlay.

I am only aware how universal the second photographic age has become because I am so often in the line of fire. This does not mean that my appearance has recently improved. It only signifies that I have become more notorious. At best the reason for taking a picture of me is that it can be sold to a newspaper, at worst it is proof that the person shown standing beside me has actually met me.

In a copy of the *Readers Digest*, I once read that the duck-billed platypus must eat twice its own weight in worms every day or it may die. The man who took the excellent picture of me used on the cover of the paperback edition of my auto-biography was the platypus of the camera. He seemed to feel compelled daily to consume his own weight in celluloid. Since meeting him I have come to realize that a great many photographers are obsessed with their occupation; they take pictures of everything. Presumably this is partly because once again cameras have become so easily portable.

When I was a model I was bewildered that the

desire to paint overtook people who could have stayed in bed all day but I saw that at least an artist has the pleasure of passing judgement on his environment and, by distortion, ruling or even defeating it. Some would say he could not help doing this. The craze for photography is even more baffling. To invent a critical vision with the aid of a camera is much harder but, having recently stood before a great many photographers, even going as high as Mr Scavullo, I have become dimly aware that they too are converting me to their own use – that deep down I am only a sentence, perhaps a mere comma – in the forever unfinished essay that each of them is writing about the visible world.

It is hardly surprising that, by some means or other, each man is trying to record his personal view of the universe. What is amazing is that nations do the same thing. There are national styles in photography. When, in England, I return at nightfall to my room, I turn on my television set without the sound. While I make my lumpy tea and green toast, I glance from time to time at the screen. When the image is American – even if it is only of a blade of grass – I know this immediately. The outline is clearer, the contrast between light and dark is stronger and the object looks more worth the money. I wonder if American photographers are redeeming my image in the same way.

The first time that I actually went on an American stage and addressed a paying audience was in Newhaven at the smaller of the two Long Wharf Theatres.

Someone had told me that this was where the plays of Mr O'Neill were originally performed. Perhaps because so many of his works have a nautical theme, I imagined that to reach the auditorium, the public would be compelled to walk along a booming wooden verandah beneath dangerously swinging hurricane lamps and that the stalls would smell of dead fish. I now saw that the two theatres and sundry other buildings were welded into a concrete structure that formed one boundary of a huge meat market. On the other side was a Howard Johnson Hotel where I stayed. From the window of my room, while I put on my stage clothes, I could watch people arriving sometimes at my theatre but more often at the larger one where *Journey's End* was being performed. Both the Long Wharf Theatres were run by a small staff of very young people who mercifully displayed the minimum of artiness and who were very friendly. Sometimes they and at other times total strangers took me round Newhaven. Wherever we went, apologies were offered for the provinciality of the environment. Had no one mentioned it, I would never have noticed. There, as everywhere I went in America, I invested everything I saw with the wonder I felt at being there at all.

Newhaven is a university town but, unlike Oxford, not affectedly so. For the most part the colleges are tactfully woven in with the surrounding architecture and the students do not look conspicuously different from real people. I went to Yale on two occasions, once at the invitation of a member of the staff and again because a rogue student asked me. On both days I was far out of my depth but remained precariously afloat on a tide of American courtesy. On my second visit I found myself among the divinity students to whom I was required to explain You-Know-Who. I began to comply with this request in a very shaky voice but soon found that, though my audience was lively, it was not disputatious. In the United States the vocabulary of undergraduates is not ostentatiously polysyllabic nor is their discourse seasoned to choking point with obscure quotations. From this entire escapade I conclude that it is the practice of American universities deliberately but in small doses to expose their inmates to the more bizarre aspects of the outer world. Experience is evidently thought to be more fortifying than mere learning.

At all first nights staged by Mr Elkins, the audience is as much under his control as the actors. The theatre is full of smiling faces, clapping hands. This is part of his method of presentation. He also carries with him on such occasions a file for bevelling the nails of critics. I could not therefore at first be sure how I was being received by America but, as my two weeks in Newhaven wore on, I began to assume a certain reciprocity in my audiences. I am not saying that every word I uttered was given a totally favourable reception but, except by the gay papers, I was seldom savaged.

From Newhaven I went to Washington and New York. There I stayed in the Algonquin Hotel, a deliberately and very charmingly old-fashioned establishment run less for profit than as a shrine sacred to the memory of that far off time when Dorothy Parker was alive and bitching. During my stay there, one of her contemporaries, Mr Connolly, was brought back from the dead to be interviewed in that very room where once stood the round table at which they sat. The first question asked of him was, 'Do you think that conversation is as witty now as it was in the good old days?' He replied, 'Mine is.'

If in the Algonquin I was given a 'good' table at breakfast time, I could be seen by all the guests who came and went in the lobby. By these means democracy was put to the ultimate test. A man came to my table and said, 'I am the congressman from Minnesota.' For a moment I feared that I had done something unconstitutional but he only wished to say a few kind words. I thanked him and he returned to his party at a distant table. If you try to imagine an English cabinet minister walking the entire length of a public place to speak to me, you will instantly see how far we have to go before we become a truly homogenized society.

In the Algonquin people talked to me for free; those who could be bamboozled into paying came to the Players' Theatre. This is situated on the western side of Washington Square, a district that has changed somewhat since the characters in Mr James's novels lived there. In London my engagement there would be comparable to appearing in Dean Street.

As soon as I saw the Players' Theatre, I thought

it the ideal place for me to work. The inside looked as though it had once been a kinky cinema. The auditorium, which held about two hundred and forty people, was long and narrow but I never had the least difficulty in being heard – even when, halfway through the run, my voice clouded over from fatigue. I never succeeded in filling the place but even a handful of people looked adequate and seemed to feel comfortable.

Until I reached New York I had always used whatever stage furniture each theatre could provide. Now the stage manager was asked to buy the required props. I was amazed at the thought that he lavished upon this small chore. For instance, when I remarked that any old chair would do, he said that it must not have a fabric seat, it must be made of something that permitted me to slide hither and thither.

'Well, yes,' I conceded, 'but, apart from that ...'

'And it must be so light that you can easily drag it forward or push it back.'

'That's true but ...'

'And it must have arms that you can lean against.'

He even bought a few ferns to make the occasion look like a Dickensian celebrity lecture.

In New York, our engagement began not with a bang but a whimper. We embarked on a series of previews to invited audiences. The purpose of these was partly to acclimatize New Yorkers to me but mostly to familiarize me, before the critics could get at me, with the shortened version of the show which Mr Elkins had translated into

American. During my first few evenings, if anything distracted my concentration while I was on stage, my lips automatically moved back into the sentences that they had become accustomed to uttering during the past three years. By the time the night of the critics had fallen, I was used to the new edition of the show.

The critics were amazingly kind to me.

Americans boast that they are a violent people and politically they are. They have killed twice as many politicians as we have murdered kings but, in the world of the theatre, both critics and audiences have velvet paws. Not even Mr Barnes denied that I was offering entertainment. Almost everybody's attitude was softened by the fact that I am a foreigner – nay, an outcast, an old man and alone. Guessing this to be so, it became difficult not to exploit my disadvantages. I stood forever on the brink of flirting with my audiences instead of performing for them. In theatrical terms this was a sin; socially it seemed to be a virtue or, to say the least, useful.

During my run at the Players' Theatre many events occurred that were surprising and some that were positively hilarious. One night, when I had been on stage for about twenty minutes, the lights began to flicker and some thumping noises issued from the wings. (Really I should say wing; it was only possible to reach the stage from one side.) Then suddenly the lights were extinguished altogether. I asked the electrician, who was lurking behind a curtain, if there just might be something wrong and he admitted that the electrical system was being rebellious. Someone in the audience suggested that we should go on as though nothing unpleasant had happened. I agreed to do this but at this moment the emergency lighting was switched on giving the place a Waterloo Station look and the owner of the building walked down the aisle to announce that the theatre was on fire. In a soothing voice he suggested that we should all leave. The mildness of his manner worked a miracle. There was no panic. Sitting on the stage, I watched everyone leave quietly as though a church service had just ended.

Almost at once an engine arrived with five firemen. Like an illustration to one of Gulliver's travels, helmeted and armed with iron pikes, these benign giants stomped on to the tiny stage. They wore boots that would have carried them through a flood.

Where two or three firemen are gathered together, there will be photographers also. Never asleep at his post, the stage manager instantly saw this occasion as an opportunity for a little publicity. He asked the Titans if they would be willing to have their picture taken with me. I have been told that the Fire Department has raised strong objections to the notion of employing known homosexuals but the invaders complied with the stage manager's request at once. The resulting picture could not be used for publicity purposes because the least suggestion that the theatre was unsafe would have been fatal but it was printed in a magazine called *Where It's At*. In brilliant lighting and holding a glass as though I were about to propose a toast, I stand before these shadowy Titans grouped in heroic postures. By a knowing eye it can just be seen that they are sending me up but so gently that together we form one of the funniest tableaux in which I have ever been involved. Every time that I look at this photograph I am surprised afresh to observe that there is a fire face. These men look more alike than most brothers. All have round, handsome faces decorated with mini-walrus moustaches and tiny laughing eyes.

Soon after this comic turn, another slighter but more enigmatic incident occurred. Someone in the audience asked if I thought that Jesus had style. I had often been questioned about You-Know-Who but very seldom interrogated about his son. As always before I talk about any religious issue, I said, 'Would anyone prefer that I did not answer this query? I wouldn't like to give offence.' Someone shouted, 'Why stop now?' so I explained that, in my opinion, the style resided either in Mr Nazareth or his biographers. This remark led me into quoting the passage from the New Testament about the woman at the well. As I began to say, 'He that drinketh of this water shall thirst again . . . ' the house seemed not only to grow quieter but also colder. This change of temperature was not lost on the stage manager. He later decided that, although it was permissible for me to express my ideas about religion in general, I must never again quote from the Scriptures. Perhaps the audience was shocked to find that anyone so wicked knew the Bible so well.

I was at the Players' Theatre for eleven weeks. By that time it was recognized by the experts that no amount of advertising could keep the show going any longer. I returned to England.

There my feeble efforts to entertain a small number of well-wishers in a tiny theatre on a dim side street in an unfashionable part of New York were described as a Broadway triumph. It has always surprised me to find that anyone at all accepts without question what the newspapers say: I was positively astonished to discover that apparently even journalists believe the outrageous statements of other pressmen.

It was impossible to define what Mr Elkins had expected not merely of my appearance in MacDougal Street but of the entire American venture. As an impresario he almost certainly succumbs from time to time to what Mr Miller calls 'the dreams that come with the territory', but in some respects he is a realist. While I was in Australia, he was in communication with Mr Cook and from him learned that no amount of publicity could inflate my poor market value to any great degree. He also knew that, in a sense, the larger the audience the less satisfying the show was bound to become because it depends on its chattiness. All the same he may secretly have hoped that we could fill a small theatre indefinitely.

In financial terms it is probable that he thought of me as a walking, talking tax loss.

What the people who came to hear me took away from the performance I have no idea. One night, during the interval, a member of the audience came up on to the stage and sat for a while in the other chair. 'What can I say?' she asked. 'What can I give you?' Before I could make out a list, she had taken from round her neck a gold chain. This she placed in my lap. What folly! What wonderful folly! Gestures of generosity such as this, the letters, the hospitality that were showered upon me have made me examine very carefully the almost mystical relationship between the solo performer and American audiences. The enigma certainly does not originate in me. I offer the world nothing but my availability – myself. The mystery must therefore spring from the United States. New York is that Aaronic rock which, if you strike it in the hope of unleashing a miracle, will reward you with a perpetual flow of love.

If I ask myself what I originally wanted from a visit to America, I can now give no reply. The fulfilment has outstripped the expectation.

When not on stage, not being interviewed by straight television or the gay press, I was being lavishly entertained – sometimes by people I had met in England, on other occasions by individuals or groups whom I knew little or not at all. These festivities usually took place in the middle of the night after the show. This was largely due to the fact that, although whenever it rains in New York it rains credit cards from heaven, most of the city's inhabitants work. In England regular employment is considered by those who can find it to be a way of winning eternal life on the principle that work tastes so nasty it must be doing you good. To Americans a job is an excuse for going out into the world where at any moment they may encounter success or, at the very worst, true love.

Almost until dawn generosity was lavished upon me as though I were a star. As Mr Auden has said, 'God bless the USA, so large, so friendly and so rich.' I was not only fed until I could hardly stand but transported in purring limousines to the homes of total strangers and returned in the same fashion to my hotel. This was common practice even when my hosts lived outside Manhattan. Just as well. I still spoke no American and have no sense of direction other than downwards. On one occasion I was even taken to and returned from Staten Island. That day it looked like a Christmas card painted by Mr Breughel. The snow was untouched by human foot and from this Tide-white surface sprang astonishingly black trees. Because the terrain is as lumpy as school porridge, my eye was everywhere greeted by a landscape either spread out beneath or towering above it. The world presented itself as artists see it with the very minimum of sky.

The sky is a mistake.

During the day I spent a certain amount of time sitting in my hotel room. Every now and again my solitude was beguilingly interrupted by telephone calls from journalists asking for my views on topics so general that even I was able to express an opinion about them.

'What do you think will happen in 1979?'

'Everything will get worse.'

'Marvellous. Thank you so much. Goodbye.'

In my mind's ear I hear a compositor speaking

on his intercommunications system to his editor

'Is that you, chief?'

'What is it now, Albert?'

'Well, I've set the piece on Pregnancy after Forty and it doesn't quite come to the bottom of the column. Shall I reset the whole thing in eighteen point?'

'How much space is there left to fill?'

'About half an inch.'

'Don't bother. It'll be cheaper to ring up Quentin.'

When not incongruously posing for the papers as one of the sages of the ages, I watched television.

In England all good television programmes have come across the Atlantic. If the men are running fast and shooting straight, they are Americans. British television tends to be as boring as being alive. Perhaps I should say as boring as life used to be.

However, when you are in New York where so many channels are available, where so many hours of the day and night have to be filled with something, monotony does sometimes flood the screen. Low tide in entertainment begins at midday and continues until about half-past four in the afternoon. In this temporal desert, five or six continuing narratives flourish like cacti on the very minimum of sustenance. They are so alike that, with practice, a viewer could switch from the question in one story to the answer in another. Each episode of each programme begins thus.

'Have you a moment to spare?' (A needless

enquiry: the entire cast has a lifetime to spare.)

'Of course, do sit down.'

'Thank you. I want to talk to you. I'm worried about Marge. I don't think Gerry is right for her.'

'Ah, if only she hadn't left Andy . . .'

Occasionally into this world of middle-brow, middle-class women, men are introduced. They are always as handsome as the sun with eyes the size of chicken's eggs and they have never in their lives taken anything seriously except a mirror. Even so, they too have opinions as to whether or not Gerry is right for Marge.

By the end of every afternoon at least three women are in hospital. They suffer from the effects of self-administered poison, self-administered alcohol or pregnancy administered by someone who isn't right for them. Day after day I sat before one of the Algonquin's television sets waiting for one of the characters on the screen to say, 'Don't you think that perhaps we should stop meddling in the lives of others?'

These words were never spoken.

Although I never ceased to send them up, I did not really mind whiling away the daylight hours with these pageants of domestic anguish. I was seduced by their unreality. The only programmes than see which I would rather do anything – even work – are those which involve real people as opposed to actors. During the most sombre stretches of television when the screen was disfigured with panels, quizzes or the news, I was frequently saved by *New York Magazine*.

To find out if it was feasible for me to work for

such an illustrious magazine, my agent took me to Second Avenue to call on a certain Miss Koenig, who rules the paper's book page. She not only found the idea acceptable but allowed me to write almost anything that came into my head and further indulged me by giving an office tea party for me just before I left America.

I also became involved in a curious subdivision of the profession of book reviewing of which until recently I had never heard. Publishers sent me uncorrected proofs of forthcoming books not exactly for criticism but rather in the hope of cajoling me into making a few favourable comments which could be woven in with other blandishments on the dust-jackets of their first editions.

Aware that I owe a great deal to the world in general and to the United States in particular, I always try to find something nice to say about whatever rubbish I am given to read. I do this partly so as not to find myself inhabiting a jungle infested with angry novelists who might snarl at me if our paths cross and partly because to produce even the slenderest volume costs money and it is therefore sacred. Even when on one occasion I was sent yet another survey on homosexuality, this time so gross that nothing commendatory could be written about it, I tried to turn my disapproval to account. After all there are many quarters where my disapprobation is considered to be praise.

I once heard someone complain that my critiques of books are less about what I have just read than about myself. I was surprised at this remark. I almost always describe a book first as a physical object: I then say something about its contents and the style in which these are presented. It is true that I quite often pause to explain why I hold the opinions to which I have given expression and, on occasion, I throw in an anecdote in which I have played some part. When working for Mr Kington of *Punch*, I do this because he has said that, from any book review, he hopes to learn something about the critic as well as about the work under discussion. When I adopt this procedure elsewhere, I do so because it seems so unlikely that any editor would solicit my ideas on the grounds that I am a literary authority; it seems much more probable that he thinks that his readers may be curious about me as a person.

Books are for writing – not for reading. Nevertheless I gladly peruse anything sent to me for review. I need the money and the fragment of publicity that accrues from signing a few hundred words in a magazine may be helpful. When I ask Mr Carter for permission to live in America forever, it must seem that I am perpetually in work. Though I would prefer to do absolutely nothing at all, I do not dislike composing pieces of prose if they are short. When I come to the end of them, I may, with luck, still be able to remember what I said at the beginning but, if I write a whole book, after a while I am overtaken by the fear that I have begun to state the opposite of what I said at the outset. I am then forced to read my first few chapters over again. I find re-reading even my own deathless prose tedious in the extreme.

The writing of books is much harder than painting even the largest picture because narrative is disposed in time rather than space. For an artist to be able to appreciate the difficulties that beset authors, he would have to imagine designing a mural that continued from one room to another. Then he would be forever running from the end of his frieze to the beginning and back again to make sure that all the details contributed in the right measure to the final effect. This is what a novelist or a biographer is compelled to do every day.

If, by now, you are weeping for me, dry your tears. The book that you hold in your hand or, possibly, have just flung on to the floor is almost certainly the last that I shall ever attempt to write.

Shortly before I left MacDougal Street someone came to my dressing-room (which was really a dance rehearsal room above the stage) and announced that he wished to make a record of the show. I was a little less disbelieving than I might have been because about two years previously I had encountered a Mr Napier-Bell who had in mind a similar but even more outlandish scheme. He wanted me to sing. This proposal I simply could not take seriously at all. My speaking voice has been described by the kinder newspapers as 'tarnished silver'. If this is an apt phrase, then my singing is like rusty tin. It has no resonance, no range, no volume. Furthermore I have no sense of rhythm or melody.

There are two main ways in which a person may find it difficult to keep in tune. He may either be unable to predict what sound will come out of his face or, if two noises have different qualities, such as a piano and the human voice, he may be quite unable to tell whether or not they have the same pitch. I suffer from both these handicaps.

All this I explained to Mr Napier-Bell on the telephone. He insisted on visiting me.

He looked like Mr Redford but without the permanent expression of suppressed contempt. He was most polite but quite determined.

Mr N-B: Everybody can sing – even you.

Me: Tra-la.

Mr N-B: You're quite right; you can't sing but you can speak a lyric.

Me: Like Mr Harrison?

Mr N-B: No. Like Miss Dietrich.

So I started off in the legendary world-weary moan to say that I was falling in love again. A likely story!

I had not uttered more than a few bars when my visitor interrupted me. 'No. That won't do,' he said. 'It's not you.'

For our experiment he had chosen a lyric made famous by Miss Lee, presumably on the principle that we should emulate the best. It was a song of mourning not for lost love but for vanished happiness. Before Mr Napier-Bell left, we had agreed that I need not imitate anyone but should intone this elegy in a voice charged with feigned emotion.

My task-master was infinitely patient. He caused the lyric to be typed out like a poem so that I could learn my lines by heart and he left with me a quaint machine no bigger than a match box on which he showed me how to play the required tune over and over and over. The difference between this elegant gadget and the huge metal box into which I had spoken words for Mr O'Connor told me how much time had passed since then. As the years rush by, people become bigger but mechanical devices get smaller.

When, as nearly as I was ever likely to, I understood what I was meant to do, a day was fixed for making a record.

In a dim basement in Denmark Street, there is a sinister room divided down the middle by a huge glass wall. The two halves of this studio can only communicate through the microphone or by sign language. In one part there is an instrument panel as complicated as that which bewildered Miss Day when she was required to land an air liner aided only by instructions from the control tower. When you hire this demon machine you are allotted a man like a gift in a packet of Shredded Wheat. He and Mr Napier-Bell sat side by side behind this science-fiction object. I went into the other half of the room. There I found nothing but a huge microphone. I stood in front of this wearing earphones through which the now horribly familiar tune assaulted my skull at discotheque level. At a sign from Mr Napier-Bell I took a deep breath. Before I had uttered a sound, I was waving my arms to indicate that we must begin again. I had not realized that every time I breathed the microphone would emit a hoarse growl. I was told this did not matter and we started afresh.

I think I did about four renderings of Miss Lee's song, before I was allowed into the other part of the room to hear one of them. Having no notion of what was expected of me I was neither shocked nor pleased by what I heard until I noticed that in the word 'never' the second syllable was inaudible. When I mentioned this defect, the man who belonged to the machine slowly dragged a switch along a groove then suddenly with the speed of light moved his hand to another switch and back again. With no more fuss than this, the word 'never' was transferred from another sound track on to the one that was considered the least feeble. I know now that a mouse could give an adequate rendering of 'Softly Awakes my Heart' if the technical staff was on her side.

Nothing ever came of the record that Mr Napier-Bell was trying so hard to make. In a way I was sorry. He was so indulgent with me that he deserved some reward. Also I hate being part of any project which is finally a dead loss to someone who has taken an interest in me but I think it is just as well that this particular dream – this particular nightmare – was never translated into fact.

The idea put forward by the man who came to my dressing-room at the Players' Theatre was a little more realistic; he only wanted to record my speaking voice. Like a fire bucket his request was passed along the chain of employees that connected me with Mr Elkins and some days later we received permission to proceed. The stage manager and I rushed straight from MacDougal Street to a nearby recording studio. This differed from the room in Denmark Street in that this time I and the microphone were in a larger room filled with conscripted listeners.

The occasion was an ordeal because, by the time the record was complete, it was well after midnight and I had been speaking for four-and-a-half hours but the evening was made worthwhile by my discovery that in the audience was Miss Comden.

When the record was released in England, to promote it I was whirled round Britain by a member of the staff of EMI. I asked him what the three mysterious letters meant and he replied, 'Every Man for 'Imself'.

Apart from New York, the only other American city in which my theatrical engagement was prolonged was Los Angeles. From the very first morning that I awoke in California, I felt abundantly well. There was a warm film of moist air lying on my face. It was as though I were living in a happy Ireland – if you can imagine anything so far-fetched. We were staying at the Beverley Hills Hotel in a splendour to which sadly I shall never become accustomed; there isn't enough time left.

My agent thought that what few spare hours were allowed to us we should spend by the swimming pool on the grounds that we might never again be where this symbol of luxury was available. I was frightened by the boiling sun and the frying people but I forced myself to be brave. My efforts turned out to be worthwhile. On a modern version of a chaise longue lay a gentleman who was revealed to be a doctor when his name was called by a telephone assistant. The instrument, on a cable of infinite length, was brought to him at once but for a long while he was obviously unable to stem the flood of words that flowed from the other end of the wire and which, try as we might, we could not hear. They evidently formed some patient's cry for help because when at last he could make himself heard, the physician said, 'I'll do my best to get around to you later in the day but we're terribly understaffed here.' He then laid the telephone down beside the pool and sank back into a recumbent posture.

I have one of my spies even in Los Angeles. When I told him where I was staying and invited him to visit me, he confessed to being intimidated by my setting but he summoned up sufficient courage to fetch me in his purring limousine and drive me to his home. Like many householders in this area he lives his entire life in that hazardous moment which occurs in all cartoon films when the victim, fleeing before his pursuers, does not notice that he has run out of land and is treading air over a bottomless abyss. My friend's house juts out horizontally from the side of a valley regardless of the fact that the earth slopes vertiginously downward below it. From his verandah in the sky it is possible with a telescope (which he has) to survey the whole celluloid kingdom. The dinky rurality that characterizes the English countryside is nowhere to be seen. The view looks like a Japanese painting; each range of mountains is green at the top but fades into a yellowish mist behind the next bright row of hills. Never before have I beheld a natural vista so beautifully conventionalized.

Apart from this delightful excursion in my friend's car most of my days were spent on Sunset Boulevard. The palm trees along either side of this legendary thoroughfare are of an astonishing height but their growth has obviously cost them a great effort; they look very tired. Once a year, as with some of the human inhabitants of the neighbourhood, an expert makes his rounds to groom them for continued stardom. Sunset Boulevard leads from the hotel to the television station where I was interviewed by Mr Snyder. To English eyes he appears blindingly handsome but in California his looks count for less because there standards are so high. Great care is taken to present not only him but his entire programme in a glamorous light. When later I saw the one in which I appeared I noticed that even I had been to some extent redeemed.

Though I have glanced fleetingly at so much geographical splendour in recent years, Los Angeles is by far the most idyllic region through which I have ever passed. There it is always summer; there happiness rains down from the sky; there pretty women and awards grow on trees. By the beginning of April the gardens of the rich are choked with roses the size of cabbages. Humming birds pause in the air above you or dart between the trees like microdot Supermen while, twice the size of these tiny creatures, swallowtail butterflies, which in England are as rare as number fourteen buses, do barre work on the edge of your breakfast table. It saddened me to see that, in spite of all this beauty, the word most often printed on the roadside hoardings was 'hypnotist' and on one occasion, 'Hip hypnotist'. It would seem that the inhabitants of this earthly paradise are not content with it. They devote a considerable amount of time and energy to attempting to enrich their environment still further. First they tried religion, then drugs, then meditation and now hypnosis.

All this cut-price transcendentalism does not prevent California from being a startlingly physical state. This becomes most obvious where Los Angeles saunters down to the sea. The region is called Venice. In the distance lies the Pacific. It is a rich swimming-pool blue and despite its terrifying vastness, it tiptoes towards the shore like a woman approaching a sleeping baby but no one ever dips so much as a lacquered toe into it. The sand, on which no child ever plays, is dented with sand pits. These are furnished with large varieties of gymnasium equipment used so continuously and with such vigour that locally there has sprung up a tribe of men who, like women of the 1890s, cannot lay their arms against their sides. This affliction restricted ladies of the Edwardian era because their ball gowns were padded under the arms. In California today it attacks the men because they have so strenuously developed their dorsal muscles. This has been done to acquire the bat's-wing silhouette so greatly to be desired.

While the males of Los Angeles widen their contours by every means possible, the females narrow theirs. New Yorkers talk about what they eat; Californians go into ecstasies over what they refrain from eating.

During our stay in this heaven on earth, we were invited by Mr and Mrs Elkins to a party at their home on Mulholland Drive. This must be the longest street in the world – the address was in five figures. Our hosts' house was made entirely of glass. Of this I approved – it placed them in the availability business too. The guests were either lawyers or actresses. Among the latter was Miss Browne who told me that giving talks to American universities could easily be converted into a way of life. She said that there are so many that by the time you have visited all of them and returned to New York for a good cry, the day has arrived to start out again. By then the students whom you have addressed so far will all have gone out into the world. I regarded this information as most heartening. It suggested a way in which I might meet more people than I had thought possible – and all without paying my fare.

As I was leaving the party, Mrs Elkins put her head into the car for a moment and said, 'I promised you America and you shall have it.'

In a way I did.

The End

Long after *The Naked Civil Servant* had been translated into a television play but before I had ever been abroad, I returned one last time to St Alban's College of Art where I had been employed intermittently for more than thirty years. I was already standing on my piece of tat in one of the 'life' rooms waiting for the housewives' choice class to begin when the first student arrived. She greeted me pleasantly and added, 'So you've come back to us.'

'Yes, madam.'

'You *were* a nine days' wonder, weren't you?'

'Yes, madam.'

In quite a long time this was the most coolly bitchy – the most English – remark that had been flung at me. Malice is in no way redeemed by being true. The past four years have obviously been band-wagon stuff. I never became, nor shall I ever become, entrenched in the public consciousness. I have not been nor shall I ever be written into even the most frivolous history of my epoch. I never worked in the centre ring of the three-ring circus of show business but, with the help of the people mentioned in these pages, I came nearer to the 'big time' than I ever dreamed I would.

I speak of all this at what to many may seem disproportionate length because I have approached the heart of the world from such a galactic perimeter; there have been so many radiation belts to penetrate and I came so totally unarmed. Nay, I can say more. Never in the history of the printed word has so much mileage been squeezed out of one flimsy book.

By the time this last instalment of my life story is published, I shall have returned to the United States. Either the musical based on my autobiography will have been produced or the project will have been abandoned. In either case, when all the public speaking and the public living are over, when the being interviewed on television and the being photographed for the papers are done, I shall make the first important decision that I have made in a long time. I shall timorously approach the immigration authorities of the United States to ask their permission to spend the rest of my life in New York. Even this dramatic change of habitat will alter my mode of being less than some might think. Wherever I am on this earth, I am and shall always be only a resident alien. People are never with me, they are always in my presence. I am never involved in conversation, I am always being interviewed.

If I am allowed to stay in America, if I can scrape together sufficient money to subsist indefinitely in the fizzy air of Manhattan, I must remember that I shall no longer be the recipient of the special attention the island has so far always bestowed upon me. I shall by then have become at least an honorary member of its divine race of denizens. It will then be my turn to dispense unfailing generosity – if not in money, then in some other currency. In other words it will be my duty to acquire and to manifest the typical American virtues.

When I was burbling on in this fashion to a BBC reporter in New York, he asked me if I did not think my attitude disloyal to Britain. I gasped but quickly converted this unsophisticated reaction to a deep breath taken before launching into a eulogy of my native land.

The question deserves a careful answer. Until recent times, on a superficial level, English society has stared at me from beneath raised eyebrows and spoken of me with thin curved lips but I must never deny that fundamentally the mildness of the British temperament, as codified in its minimum risk laws, is what has made it possible for me to survive into old age. For many years, in spite of pathological laziness and conspicuous lack of talent, I have been permitted to earn a living somehow. Now I am kept by the state for which, unlike Mr Othello, I have done no service. In Russia, in China, in Cuba, I would long ago have been shot – or worse.

Britain cherishes her eccentrics and wisely holds that the function of government is to build a walled garden in which anarchy can flourish. The entire island is a home for incorrigibles where the very young, the very old and those, who, from any cause whatsoever, feel ill-equipped to live will be protected. For these reasons, though I make fun of England with every breath I draw, I have never seriously criticized her.

Unfortunately I am living my later years with their time factor reversed. I ought to have crossed the Atlantic in early middle age and should now be coming home to die but thirty years ago my poverty and my general ineffectuality prevented me from attempting a journey so daring. Now, in the winter of my life, I have been carried across the ocean as though on a plate. This astonishing piece of good fortune I must not waste.

Perhaps the wisest course of action for me to adopt will be to lie down on the White House steps and, when the occupant opens the door, to start whimpering those lines engraved round the plinth of the Statue of Liberty: 'Bring me your huddled masses yearning to breathe free . . .'

If ever there was a huddled mass . . .